Animal Drawing

ANIMAL DRAWING

by

Frank Medworth

Faber and Faber Limited
24 Russell Square
London

First published in November mcmxxxiv
by Faber and Faber Limited
24 Russell Square London W.C.1
Reprinted in mcmxliv and mcmxlviii
Printed in Great Britain by
Gilmour and Dean Limited Glasgow and London
All rights reserved

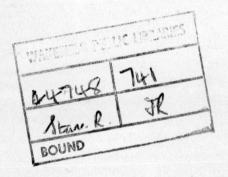

Preface

FOR SOME YEARS I CONDUCTED A CLASS OF PUPILS IN ANIMAL Drawing at the London Zoological Gardens, and during this period the subject became very absorbing to me.

That loving an object makes that object seem more worthy is but one of those strange truths which intrigue the thoughtful person. Contemplative observation truly endears the animals to us; and no finer method of observing may be found than that watchful one necessary to the draughtsman. He must exercise both patience and courage. Patience in investigation and choice of moment, and fearlessness in drawing the essentials. These essentials are not the same to everybody and one must become sometimes unscrupulous, sometimes as though possessed by an unearthly exhilaration, but always with that humbleness which man experiences when before an immaculately conceived living creature.

It is hoped that the collected notes in this book may serve as a guidance in directing the interest of a few towards that vast field of study embraced in the words Animal Drawing. Also, that they will facilitate an easier approach than would be possible to many coming quite freshly to this study.

June 1935.

F. C. M.

Contents

Illustrations
other than diagrams

Animal Drawing

Chapter 1

Bears

DRAWING ENLARGES ONE'S POWER OF VISION: IT CREATES A
larger world.

The draughtsman sees an object intimately and thereby develops powers of observation. The habit of selection requisite
to good drawing makes the student analytical and develops his
memory.

These notes on animal drawing are suggested as a course of
training in acquiring draughtsmanship and, in that fundamen-
tals are stressed to the exclusion of mannerisms, should assist the
student in seeing, memorising and symbolising with equal facility.

Bears have been chosen as a first exercise because of their appearing more simple in form—admitting of a summary approach. Both the heavy form and the thick hair contribute to a
bigger, unbroken mass than with other animals, besides showing
fewer anatomical incidents.

Diagram 1 on page 17 shows a line running the whole length
of the back to the tip of nose. This is the most significant line in
any animal or attitude and should be studied from life.

Diagram 2 gives the next stage and shows lines symbolic of the
forward edges of fore and hinder limbs. These are considered as
starting from, at top, their junction with the barrel of the body.

Diagram 3 shows the limbs drawn through to the far side and
the barrel completed with under side of head and neck. The importance of tracing through the far side limbs will be perceived on
reflecting that the gait of animals differs considerably. Whether

15

the action gives movement diagonally or rakes both sides *alternately* is of prime value in portraying successfully any animal. It is a matter for keen observation and severe self training for the draughtsman.

In Diagram 4 will be seen shading added to the undercutting lines. All underneath lines and those in any way turned under have been darkened. This will give a ready means of noting the third dimension. The shading may be done with a mere rubbing of the finger or a slower, more careful pencil hatching: though the adoption of a means towards rapidity of execution is advised. Although these figures are of a bear, the same approach might be made in noting the peculiarities of any animal, and the four diagrams should be accounted as introductory.

Diagram 5, showing a three-quarter front and top view, has the nearest contours darkened; as though the right-hand sides of curves seen in Diagram 3 are turned towards the spectator. There has been, also, a little amplification in the interest of completion. It will be noticed that the figure depends, for its legibility, on the placing of the new outlines. This manner of notation will admit of considerable development.

One might very well take the vertical section lines of a boat as a basis for investigation: midships, a section cut through at the greatest fulness of the ribs (A); prow or nose will be ignored and a little in and towards midships or barrel will be taken—a section from top of shoulder to wrist (B). Stern will be taken as through top of quarters to outside of heel (C). Diagram 6 gives, to left of centre, midships to stem; whilst the right hand side shows the stern elevation.

Note that the shoulder is higher than barrel and that quarters are lower than barrel. These differences, if noted when drawing, will go far to *specially* characterise animals.

16

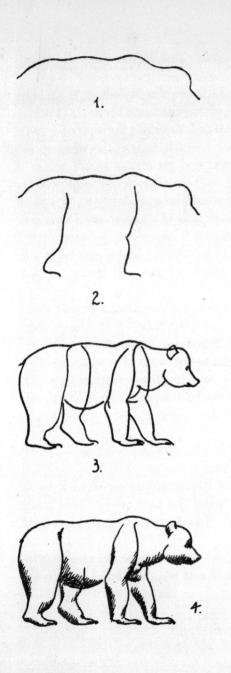

1.

2.

3.

4.

5.

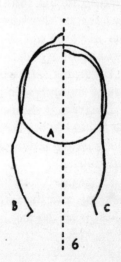

A

B   C

6.

With some animals the quarters are higher than the shoulders.

If one were to get down on all fours, the thumbs to the inside, there would be several points of resemblance between this attitude of the human and the normal standing position of a bear. The *radius*, that lower arm bone which ends at the wrist on the thumb side, would have crossed and given the *radial action* of the fore limb of quadrupeds; and, because of the fingers being longer than the thumb, there would be a tendency for the hand to turn inwards. This action is typical of those animals with unretractile or semi-retractile claws. The elbow, or head of the *ulna* (the outside bone of fore-arm), would be cast outwards slightly. This because of the weight of the body being, in part, taken on the arms.

Diagram 7 shows the bony axes of the human arm in the before-mentioned position and Diagram 8 the fore-leg of a bear; these are seen from behind. Lines A show axial directions of both.

In passing, attention is drawn to the 'arch of support' ever recurring in the construction of mobile forms. Nature sees to it that the architecture shall always be adequate to her needs; and one must be apt to recognise the needs and the suitability of form to those ends.

Diagrams 7-10 will show this arch-like construction—the left side of the arch seen from the back.

Diagram 9 shows an arch of the saracen form—the knee *of the human* being cast outwards and the heel raised. This is also the walking action of the bear. The *os calcis* or heel bone is off the ground.

Diagrams 11 and 12 give side views of fore and hinder comparisons, and the arch is made in one with the hand and, in the other, with the foot.

18

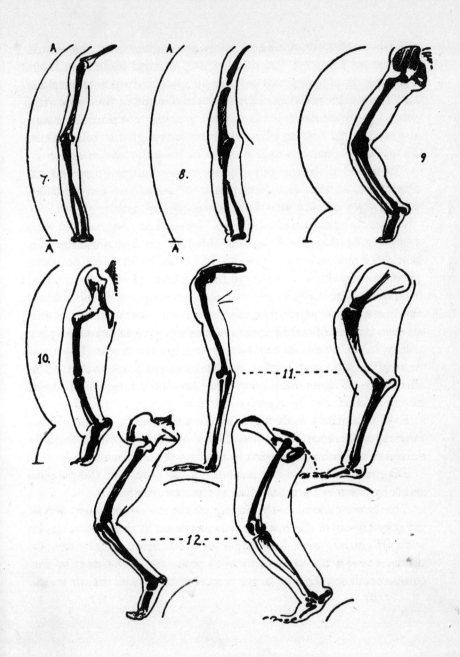

Plans of the feet of a bear (the bony structure) will be seen in Diagrams 13 and 14. The *meta carpal*, or hand bones, are shown bounded by a strong curved line at their forward extremities and denote the position of greatest movement in the hand. The other line indicates less movement and the dotted line is suggestive of still less capacity of action although the joints exist. The same might be noted of the *meta tarsal* or foot bones.

These two diagrams show at their natural angles, fore and aft. The claws, as with most animals, are hooked and have sectionally a longer upright axis than that across the nail.

A plan of the whole animal will be seen in Diagram 15 with arrows indicating the directions of feet in normal standing position. Also the ears and eyes should be noted for their positions on and in the skull. The curved lines at bases of ears give normal insertions. The right eye is drawn as a triangle in order to show the three factors governing the surround to this feature. As will be seen in the following diagram, the top edge of orbit in upper part of skull forms the superior, or top, border of eye. The nasal bone gives the inner border, whilst the cheek bone will give the third edge. If these main boundaries are noted carefully, the eye of any animal may be drawn with ease.

Eyes of animals were often, in the past, drawn as though belonging to humans. This should be avoided for nothing looks so stupid as a human expression in the face of an animal.

Diagram 16 is from the skull of a polar bear, and the pattern made by the teeth is interesting to the draughtsman.

The lower canine teeth, fitting inside the upper ones, are so arranged because the lower jaw is narrower at front than upper jaw. Of course, both jaws taper towards front. There are six teeth between the canines in both jaws, and those next to the canine teeth are slightly larger than the other small incisor teeth.

20

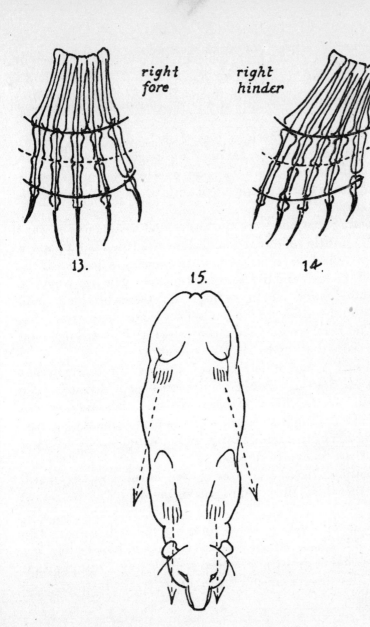

right fore

right hinder

13.

14.

15.

Diagram 17 shows what might be expected from the dropping of the lower jaw. That black lip is of special interest to the draughtsman, because of its significant form, coupled with the local colour difference, giving a characteristic of high graphic importance.

Diagram 18 gives mean sections of the hinder limbs—the two ellipses, turned outwards, having their longer axes *forwards*. A pictorial illustration (not to be taken as selectively or pictorially ideal) of this, a characteristic of all animals, is seen below in the same figure.

Supposing that one were the cutter and designer of a bear's covering, a little reflection would show that the easiest pattern to follow would be to make the main cutting edges down the centre of the back and the centre of the belly. The legs would be inserted to shoulder and top of thigh. The seams for these would be made on the insides of the limbs. Feet would be inserted, also, whilst the head would have a centre seam. This arrangement would ensure that the whole had symmetry.

With such a mass of hair as covers the bear it is of the utmost importance that one should realise these main divisions. The effect will be to facilitate the selection of essentials and give confidence in handling the design. It is possible to indicate any portion or action of the animal unerringly, should one be aware of these surface changes of the coat.

As the fur covers the muscles in their broad grouping, it will be clear that this is the outward and visible symbol of the inward motive.

Diagram 19 shows a sketch from a small Indian bear. The texture of the hair has not been insisted upon, but the *divisions* and *directions* of growth have been stated freely. Perusing from the head downwards one might see the collar, the mastoid group

22

16.

17.

18.

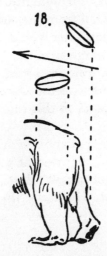

(*the mastoideus* is that strong muscle which, arising from behind the ear, divides and is inserted partly at base of neck and partly around the elbow) and the shoulder group.

The grizzly and brown bears often have a mass of hair like a saddle on top of shoulders and partly down the *dorsal* or middle part of back. Particularisation had best be acquired in drawing from the animals as this treatise would become too long should we enumerate all the possible varieties.

Tufts from the elbows, to radiate to wrists and to cover the mittens, are resembled in reverse by the hinder leg.

In Diagram 20 will be seen the longer tufted hair which occurs frequently on the polar bear. The hinders seem to be encased in trousers with frayed bottoms. Also the claws emerge from amongst quite long tufts of hair. This, in a wild state, would prevent slithering on the ice. The claws of the polar bear do not normally touch the ground.

Diagram 21 gives a portion of a polar bear. The mastoid group is very apparent and there is a radiation of hair from around the *obicularis oris* surrounding the mouth. The hair, otherwise, is designed to fall from the shoulders backwards and downwards in the way that water would separate and, no doubt, this action is intended as suggestive.

It is hoped that the scientific anatomist will not prove that the bear possesses no such muscle as the *obicularis oris*—at least he has something to correspond to this muscle on the face of the 'lord of creation'.

Diagram 22 shows the radiation of hair (from centre, outwards and posteriorly) on the head of a grizzly. The same arrangement will be true of almost all animals. The bear snarls and his nose is wrinkled. The black lip is here seen and the mouth pattern of teeth.

24

19.

20.

21.

Diagram 23 gives another grizzly bear: the eyelid will be noted, the hair on which radiates consistently with the general planning.

In Diagram 24 will be seen the 'seam' up the inside of the right fore-arm of a grizzly. The action is that of striking and the pads on the under side of foot are indicated.

No animal may be satisfactorily rendered without due attention being paid to surface texture. The difference in length or growth of hair will show differently reflected or transmitted light and should be studied by those who intend to become finished masters.

Diagram 25 gives the direction of hair on the head of a grizzly bear. The frontal shape of the head is covered with shortish hair, down the nose and around the muzzle. One might expect this to be lit on those contours towards light and shadowed oppositely. As the hair descends the nape of neck and onto shoulders there is an area of hair that stands upright on the form. This will appear light in a dark surround, or dark if the surrounding areas are light. There would be a tendency for the hair to darken otherwise (where rather long) towards the light and to transmit the light to those surfaces raked by the light.

Hair texture is seen under two conditions of lighting in Diagrams 26 and 27.

There is a further element which must not be overlooked when drawing animals. It is that of the 'break' or the channels between clogged tufts of hair. The hair is either matted by the extreme greasiness, exuded from the body glands, or clogged after bathing.

These breaks occur most noticeably at the elbow junction of ribs, at the lower end of *femur* junction with the barrel, around

26

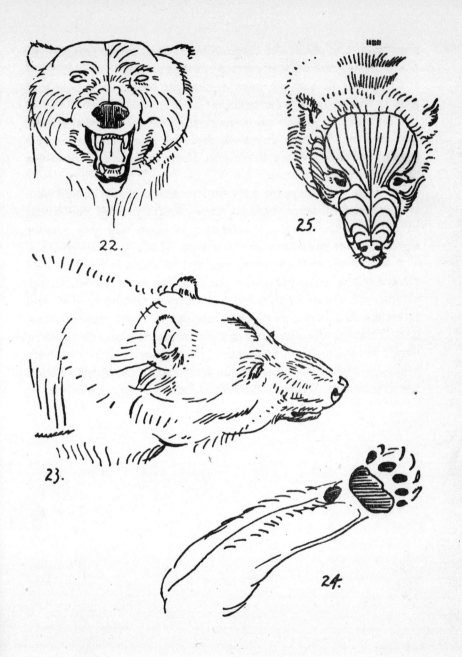

22.

25.

23.

24.

the throat and inside the thigh. Those of the throat encircle the under part of the neck as a series of ruff-like rings.

Diagrams 28 and 29 show systems of breaks at shoulder of grizzly and pelvis of polar bears.

The break might be taken as giving that section of the form qualified by the hair direction, and the diagrams give arrow strokes indicating these directions. There is always a bias in the direction of hair growth.

As these breaks appear only on live animals, one should note the systems of arrangements very carefully from the living model. Also the adequate designing of these will give greater significance to the active form than would otherwise be possible.

A few words as to grouping will not be amiss at this, the conclusion of the more particular studies. The word particular, applying to the individual, one should suppose the group of several to be not so particularised or to require so much incidentalisation. This is profoundly true in a pictorial sense, and the student would be well advised to practise group drawing from the basis of the group design. This may be afterwards subdivided: though not so minutely divided as to detract from the bigger motive.

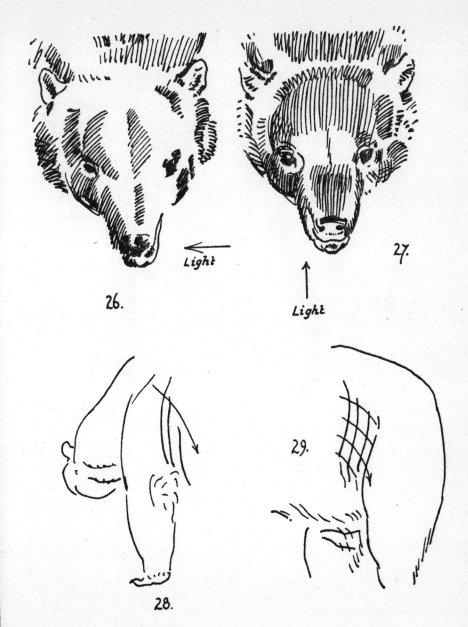

26.

Light

27.

Light

29.

28.

Chapter 2

Dogs

STUDENTS OF ANIMAL DRAWING MUST DEVELOP THE DESIRE for investigation and use every opportunity in drawing from the living form, both relaxed and in action.

It is advised that form is of first importance and, as a discipline, ought to be studied as a separate thing from light and shade, texture or values.

In the pursuit of a sound progressive method of study one might divorce pattern or shape from modelling or light and shade. Pure line more easily renders silhouette or contours than it will describe mass or form: and though it be true that choice of medium must, in some part, dictate one's technique, separate study of those things pertaining to mass (or plane boundaries) and those others having to do with realising the form (or modelling) will do much to clarify the student's analyses.

Textures, whether of actual hair growth or of the appearance of the hairy covering under different conditions of lighting, ought to be considered as separate studies. Again, the local colour markings might, advantageously, be examined and memorised with equal science.

The foregoing order is maintained throughout this book, though some additions of anatomical, comparative and formal (that relating to form) explanations have been made.

It is believed that understanding is essential to the artist, and the unhindered study of the several contributing factors of the whole should permit of a rapid notation which. in practice, often influences one's style.

'Modelling' will be used henceforth to signify those areas which are ordinarily described as 'shading'. For shading seems to suggest shadow and the existence of some light.

'Values' will describe the textural reaction to light or, to put it more simply, will show the way that some textures reflect, whilst some allow light to pass through them.

This chapter will deal with dogs.

It will be observed in Diagram 1 that a similar approach to that on the bear has been made. Line *A-A*, from tip of nose to end of tail, has been drawn first. Afterwards, the forward contours of limbs, from their junctions with mass of body. The underneaths, backward lines and further limbs were done next, and the undercutting edges darkened. It is not pretended that the modelling represents the shadow area on a dog with any given lighting; merely a dark has been taken in from the outlines on the under sides. This method is calculated to give confidence to the student in that his drawings will appear less map-like and more solid.

Diagram 2 shows a three-quarter view of the same animal as Diagram 1, seen from the front. The near contours (those toward spectator) have been darkened.

If one takes Diagram 1 and cuts vertically through shoulder to ground, again at lower end of thorax and at hind-quarters to ground, the three sections thus given would be as *A, B, C* in Diagram 3.

Diagram 4 gives the proportions of a normal dog type: namely any not malformed for some special purpose, as are bull-dogs, pugs, dachshunds and many lap-dogs and fashionable animals. The length of head, from tip of nose to back of cranium is the unit and, although the diagram is drawn as a side elevation, these proportions, subject to the foreshortening in space of any

32

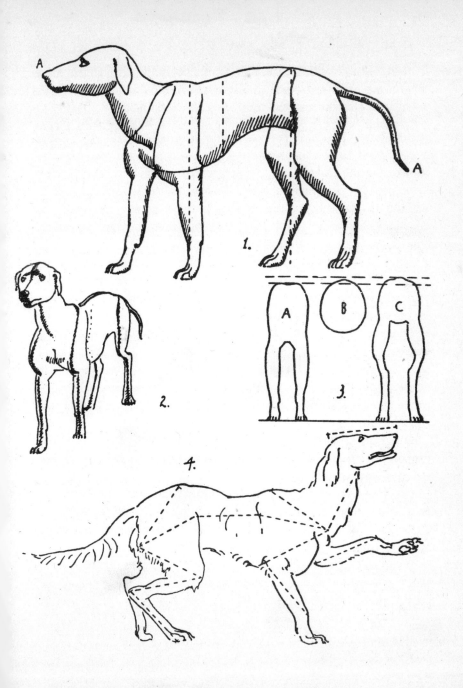

A

A

1.

A B C

3.

2.

4.

part, will be found useful in calculating many views and attitudes.

Although there is considerable movement in all parts of the structure, some parts might be regarded as being less amenable to outside influence. The *pelvis* is, for all practical considerations, a rigid mass. The thorax or chest, whilst capable of some movement, may be likened to a wicker basket in its retention of the basic cage form which flattens slightly as the animal stretches full length on the ground. Again, except for the slithering of the shoulder-blades over the ribs, the mass of the shoulders should be taken as remaining constant to section.

This knowledge prepares one for the developments in Diagrams 5-8. The dotted sectional contours show normal positions and the continuous lines give the alterations imposed by the level ground, upon which the animal is lying.

Diagram 5 is a plan-section of a dog, taken at about half-way down the ribs, and gives the altered contours. It will be noted that the cage of the ribs remains though the other masses on the one side conform to the ground plane. This makes all the contours at about twice their normal distance in projection (from the ground).

Diagram 6 shows average vertical section of hind-quarters (dotted) with the usual position when lying on the ground—marked as a straight line.

It is interesting to note the unavoidable action of crossing the two limbs: also the turning of the underneath side upwards—the vertical axis through pelvis of this view changes as dotted straight line.

Diagram 7 gives a similar section of the fore-quarters with their consequent change in the lying position. Once more the axis is changed and the legs are crossed. Also, the action of rest

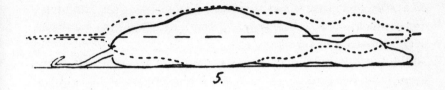

5.

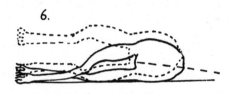

6.

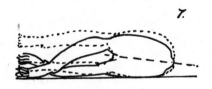

7.

requires a relaxing of the muscles which erect the lower joint—the wrist is bent.

Diagram 8 will be of interest in showing the contours of shoulders and head. The head has turned sideways in order to accommodate itself to the plane of the ground and the ears will arrange themselves as in diagram.

The importance must here be stressed of drawing the *whole animal*. Slight sketches need only be slight in their negation of everything but essentials. The effort required to draw the whole animal will tend to increase power of expression. The swift drawing, also, will often contain more action than the slower ones. These latter appear 'tired' by their lacking the rapidity of execution which, analogically, represents life.

In this manner the figures in Diagram 9, though slight, are complete.

This habit of scribbling gives understanding of the whole, and it rarely happens that one is able to draw the whole without having corresponding power over details. Moreover, as the object in drawing is to be able to draw from memory finally, constant rapidity of execution will enable one to memorise more possible views and to understand form better thereby.

The figures in this diagram demonstrate the truth of the argument offered in Diagrams 5-8. The animal is a young timber wolf in spring and the winter coat has not all disappeared from the back and hind-quarters.

To draw with freedom, one must be acquainted with certain anatomical facts. This notwithstanding the prevalent tendency to draw without understanding.

The most convincing draughtsman will himself have convictions, and the elimination of unnecessary detail should be an intellectual effort, and not the result of ignorance.

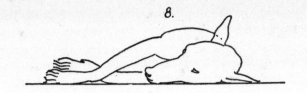

8.

9.

DOGS   The structure of the greyhound has been chosen as giving the proportions of the dog skeleton.

Diagram 10 gives a side elevation of the proportions of the body and limbs. The dotted line on the rib-cage shows the position of greatest eminence. There are thirteen ribs, attached to the *dorsal vertebræ*, and the eight true ones are more vertical in section, as seen in Diagram 11. The upright spines of the *vertebræ*, or backbones, commence at the first *dorsal* with backward leaning and then change gradually to a forward lean as far as the end of the *lumbar region*. This allows greater upward bend than downward; *i.e.* the back can be rounded more than hollowed. The apex of possible curve is at the most upright spinous process.

There is, allowed by the backward thrust of the ribs downwards, a considerable opening or arch to the cavity of the thorax —almost half of the length is free of breast bone.

Diagram 11 gives an inner line through ribs to indicate junction of ribs with cartilage: this form gives maximum capacity of expansion and contraction.

Diagram 12 shows axes of several ribs from front to rear. It will be seen that number 1 is small (at neck) and that, progressing to the 8th, there is increase in both outward and downward directions. The sides of the cage at the first few ribs show as flatter, less curved than tops and bottoms and the longer axis of cage is vertical. This slight flattening gives a surface over which the shoulder will glide easily. The false ribs (attached by cartilage to the eighth and last true rib) are higher and more curved. The diagram has dotted lines which give the curves of attachments to cartilage.

The *pelvis* at top (the *ilial spine*) *A*, Diagram 10, is just higher than the posterior end of thorax. The knee is nearer the ground than the elbow; *B* and *C*, respectively, in Diagram 10.

38

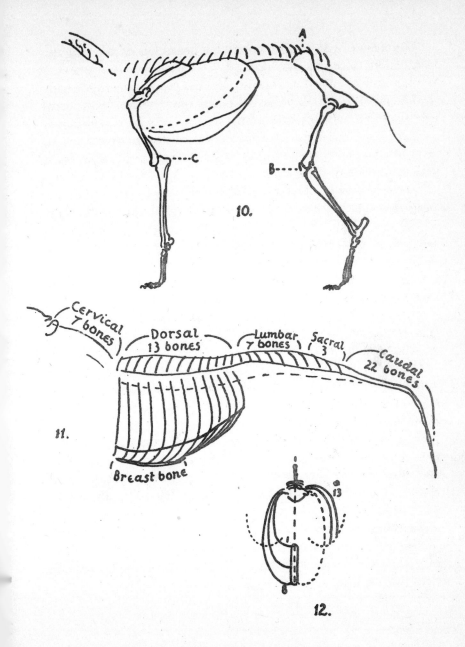

10.

Cervical
7 bones

Dorsal
13 bones

Lumbar
7 bones

Sacral
3

Caudal
22 bones

11.

Breast bone

12.

13

Diagram 13 shows the transverse directions of the ribs and transverse spines of *lumbar* section of backbone (the loins). It will be noticed that the spine of pelvis, *A*, makes a similar angle, with backbone, as these last. Dotted line through *B* indicates the direction through knee joint.

The dog's fore-leg is, as compared with the human kind, always in the prone position, that is, the thumb and *radius* are to the inner border of the limb.

The arch form demonstrated in the chapter on bears is present in all life; though more gentle in the dog than the bear. Complementary limbs will make complete arches (as also the ribcage) and, as strength is required for movement as well as support, the return of curve in limbs to some other part of the structure is essential. This re-establishment or re-attachment of curve is noticeable throughout the bony skeleton.

Diagram 14 gives a few of these returns which make for springiness in action.

Diagram 15 shows, in two figures, the front views of fore and hind limbs: the curves at hand and foot are interesting (dotted lines). The arch across both of these, shown in plans *A*, *P*, may be compared with those in humans at hand and instep sections, to which they correspond.

B gives side elevation of head of *tibia*, or true leg bone, with plan section of same. It will be noted that there is considerable rounding forwards of this head. This permits, in conjunction with ball and socket joint at top of thigh, extreme movement in the hinder limb.

Before leaving the bony understructure, several notable things about the head must be regarded. This consists of the *cranial* space, or brain cavity (somewhat oval in form) and the front part or face.

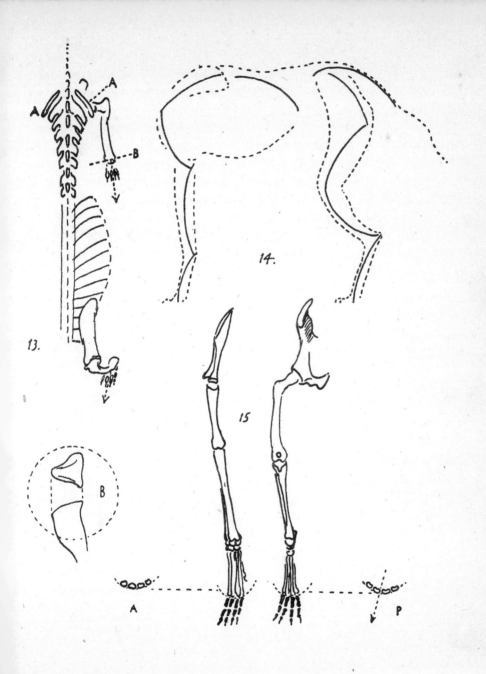

13.

14.

15.

B

A

P

Although the shape of head is determined largely by the muscular covering, the skull gives character to the individual type of dog.

The *superior* and *inferior maxillaries* are the two jaws, upper and lower; and the fore part of the upper one is worthy of notice. With the true dog, something like half only of length from 'bent' to tip of nose is bone. The bent is the downward bend of bone at the junction of *frontal* with nose bone.

As will be seen in Diagram 16, the projections which are formed by the bony setting of the back teeth of upper jaw, in conjunction with *malar* or cheek bone (Z in diagram), resemble the undercutting bows of a boat.

That projection above *orbit* or eye socket is called the *post orbital process*, and it is over this that the eyebrow proper is laid.

The study of the teeth patterns of both jaws will lead to an intelligent interpretation of the head. Fitting the *canines* or tearing teeth, with the other front incisors, will be found helpful in making drawings for snarling or menacing animals, etc. The tapering of the lower jaw towards front is general with most animals, and it will repay the draughtsman to be observant, in this respect, of varieties, when studying dogs.

Diagrams 16 and 17, giving skull and head of greyhound, show influence of various projections on surface.

Another view of upper jaw and head is given in Diagrams 18 and 19. Note the triangular setting of eye and length of cartilage and muscle of nose beyond insertion at bone.

The movement of an animal is controlled mathematically by the conditions of length, angles and articulating surfaces of bones as actuated by the 'give and take' functions of the various opposing muscles.

The student would be well advised to study a movement from

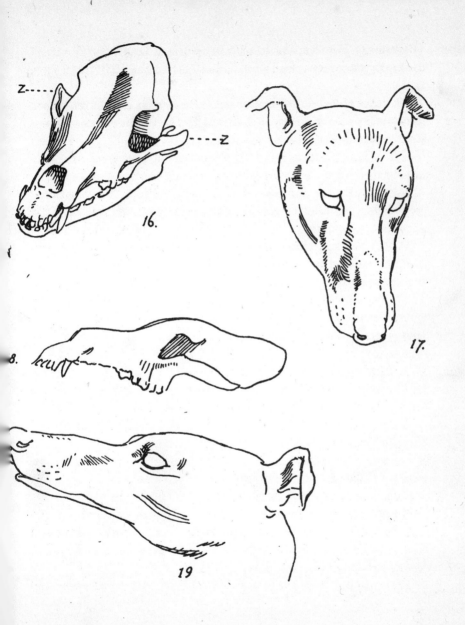

Z-----

-----Z

16.

17.

8.

19.

the basis of his own reaction to the combined parts of the action. It were better to be incorrect than to give meticulous definition of anatomical similitude. The aim should be to create an emotion rather than to state a number of irrelevant facts. One ought, perhaps, to combine several almost instantaneous phrases—the continuous motives of several moments.

The Japanese draughtsmen have sometimes rendered continuous movement by including in one design a number of checked attitudes. A flight of birds, for instance, has been conveyed by a number of similar birds showing slightly dissimilar actions; all relative to the complete action of flying.

It will be clear that the action of running or of jumping cannot be depicted by drawing the legs alone. The whole frame is engaged, and the head, ears and tail are no less expressive than the remainder of the animal.

One might so conventionalise the attitudes, or parts of them, as to be adequate to the story, though the truest symbol will be *abstracted* by the keen observer after much study: for many parts of the action would be superfluous.

It is to be remembered that choice in the draughtsman means strength; choice of 'when' no less than 'what'.

A few diagrams will be seen, on page 45, descriptive of a running and jumping dog.

Diagram 20 shows that interesting action of the hinder feet placed in advance of the fore-feet.

Diagram 25 is, supposedly, the final stage in the movement; when resumption of attitude Diagram 20 would be possible.

A convenient symbol should be used for noting hair texture—direction and quality of growth and those alterations of texture occasioned by various emotions.

There is another means by which one might characterise

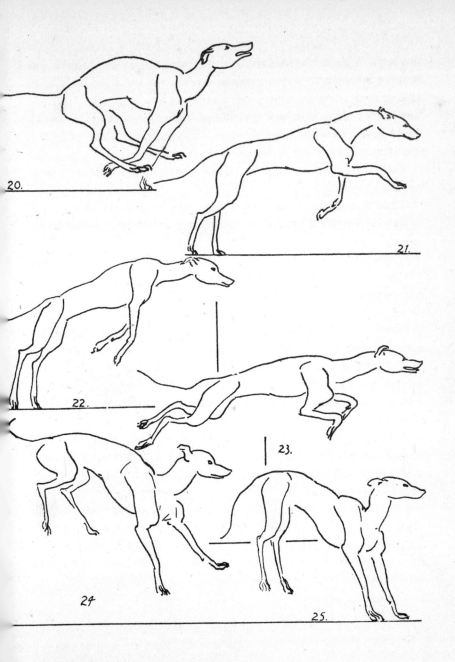

20.

21.

22.

23.

24

25.

animals. This is the colour—not the local colour so much as the accented portions. For instance, with most wild animals (and the same is inherited by their domestic descendants) the belly and under sides of head, throat and the insides of limbs are all paler in colour—they are lighter. The upper and outer surfaces are dark. This, whilst serving as a means of disguising the animal in its natural surroundings, gives to the form an appearance of great elegance.

This protective coloration, which is general with all animals, will, if understood by the draughtsman, go far to assist in creating lucid symbols.

The animal which is, for some obscure reason, darker on the under sides appears to be strangely over-pigmented.

Colour of another kind is to be seen in the eye, nose and mouth. Diagram 26 shows the importance of noting these features. The drawing is of a Samoyed dog. The animal is an albino, and the accented features become significant because of their *colour*.

Animals are not dissemblers, and the various features contributing towards any emotional expression should be studied, both separately and in combination in order to understand their degrees of importance.

A few simple diagrams will serve to show how the ears and tail, if not more voluntarily controlled than the other features, are at any rate very important media of fluent expression, expressing what the dog feels.

Diagram 27, *A* and *B*, represent the rather nervous, highly strung sort of dog. *A*, having ears and tail erected, is suggestive of interrogation; whilst *B* gives the additional information that the dog lacks confidence. The tail and ears, being at variance, intensify the expression of bewilderment to something approaching dismay.

46

26.

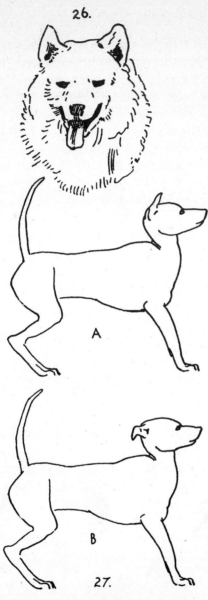

A

B

27.

Usually, downright things like fear and fury, courage, etc., are best expressed by such combination of features as will convey the sense of accumulated attributes of similar nature. Thus Diagram 28, *C*, symbolises the expression of interest, by the dog, in something. The leaning forwards on both sets of limbs, the tail erected stiffly and the ears pricked forward, together convey great concentration on some urgent matter.

This emotion is changed to one of watchful menace in *D*, Diagram 28, and one becomes aware of the readiness of the animal to bound forward at the first suspicion of weakening or danger in the cause of his anxiety.

The three figures seen in Diagram 29 convey the expression of waiting—not of resting only, but of being ready.

E has the additional quality of patience expressed; *F* is watchfully alert; *G* is in play and could, easily, be romping with a ball.

As will be appreciated, combinations of this sort are without end.

Before leaving 'man's first friend' it will be worth while to enumerate the various features. These are given in structural order, for no one is more important than the rest. It is to be remembered that these are features of *expression*: movement has been dealt with earlier.

Firstly, there is the back: it is flexible and can be rounded, hollowed, stiffened or relaxed at will.

Secondly, the legs: they not only carry the animal, but can be strutting, sagging, stiff, creeping, prancing or performing any number of other antics in as many moments.

Thirdly, the tail: it is (we are led to believe by a well-known wit) the sign of a dog's sanity. Friendship is signified by wagging the tail. It may be erected, dropped, waved, kinked at will, a very potent means of expression.

48

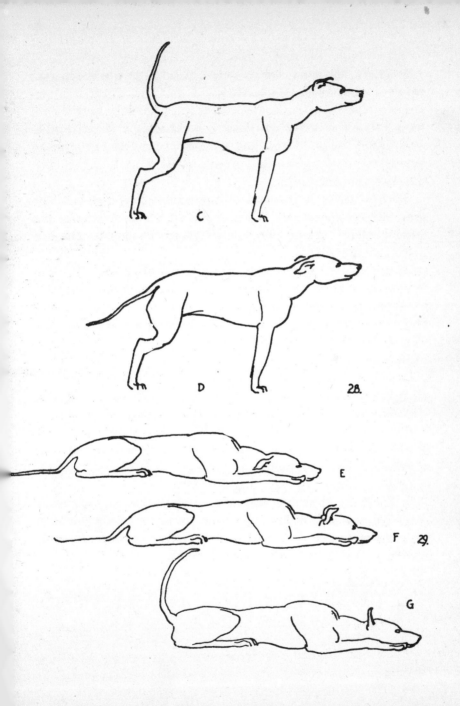

C

D
28.

E

F 29.

G

Fourthly, the jaws: these may be opened to permit the tongue to loll or when baring the teeth.

Fifthly, the snarling and elevating muscles of the nostrils and mouth: the lips are drawn back from the teeth as prevention from injury when biting. The muscles of the face can alter an expression much more subtly than can the other features, with the exception of the eye.

Sixthly, there is the ruff or that collar formation of hair around neck and throat. This, of course, serves to protect the animal when fighting; for when engaged in disputes the dog erects this matt of hair.

Seventhly, the ears: these are sure indication of awareness. By reason of their almost involuntary reaction to the slightest sound these members provide many attitudes of great illustrational value. They can be laid back (probably a further instinctive action) which serves to protect these appendages from the teeth of an adversary.

Eighth and lastly, there are the eyelids. These can show the direction in which the animal is looking, or, by being raised or lowered will expose or obscure the eyes in many subtle ways.

Diagram 30 shows the head of a snarling, wild dog. Those muscles between and below the eyes lift the lips, and in doing so wrinkle in several places, corrugating the nose and emphasising the open jaws by repeating the upward drawn line of lip.

In Diagram 31 will be seen the entirely opposite expression of friendliness and content. The eyes are partly covered by lids, the snarling muscles are not actuating lips, the ears are relaxed, and altogether there is not a trace of agitation.

30.

31.

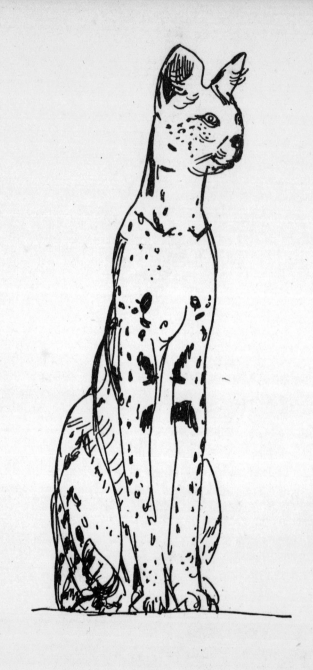

Chapter 3

Cats: Domestic, Leopard, Lion, Tiger, Ocelot, Serval

THERE IS AN IDEA CURRENT THAT, WHILE DOGS ARE MASCU-
line in character and behaviour, cats are feminine. It arises, no
doubt, from the separate tastes and friendships of the two kinds.

Dogs are more continuously active, more sport-loving and de-
structive than cats, who, generally, love comfort, are fastidious,
and insinuate gentleness, if not perhaps always possessing that
virtue.

Although these characteristics cannot be said to assist the
draughtsman, one point can be made by the comparison. The
dog is, so to say, tailored to fit, whilst the cat's covering hides
the form considerably. (Herein lies the cat's claim to femininity?)
This will be acknowledged by anyone who has seen a cat satur-
ated with water—after swimming or having been drowned.
Whether or not the animal's movements are no longer possible
in these cases, so making recognition difficult, the fact is that at
these times he is almost unrecognisable. At any rate, one's knowledge of form will have to be considerable to make easy recognition possible.

It is more difficult to express the cat, by means of elevation,
than any other animal: its back is so flexile and the character of
the animal is shown very largely by attitude. The potentialities
of spring, contained within its sinuous form, seem to be intensi-
fied by the local colour markings and make necessary a close
observation of these factors before one may hope to draw the cat
with any degree of facility.

53

Mr. Kipling's title to the story *The Cat that walked by Itself* is reminiscent of all cats and might be taken as symbolic of difficulties in drawing the animal.

Commencing with the domestic cat, which is probably a descendant of the Egyptian, crossed at intervals with native wild cats, Diagram 1 shows side view of line of back and the limbs drawn through. In places the fur has been taken for edge in order that the familiar outline should be maintained. The under cutting edges have been darkened, as advisable for this first note. It will be noticed that the hinder limbs are taller than the fore limbs, which is proper to the animal with such great powers of springing.

Diagram 2 gives a plan of a cat in an attitude similar to Diagram 1. The soft fur of the cat makes it no easy matter to separate the subcutaneous bone from muscle, or to be able to see either through the coat. The darker parts in diagram show the influence of bony structure from top side of a cat, and the thickened outlines mark the effect of bones on edge contour.

The arrows show centres of feet directions.

Diagram 3 shows sectional elevations, taken at points as indicated on Diagram 1—at *A* and *C*, and *B* gives section minus the coat.

The head of the cat is oval and this egg is roundest in the small cats and long in the largest cats.

A glance at the skeleton of a domestic cat would reveal a very delicate piece of construction. The smallness of the skull with its compacted continuity of all lines; the comparatively small thoracic cavity; the *flow* of the backbone; length of bones in the hinder limb; the tail and *sacral* region of equal length to that of *lumbar* and *dorsal* regions together; the very large shell-like sheath to the claws; are all remarkable in their obvious intention to serve adequately their several purposes.

54

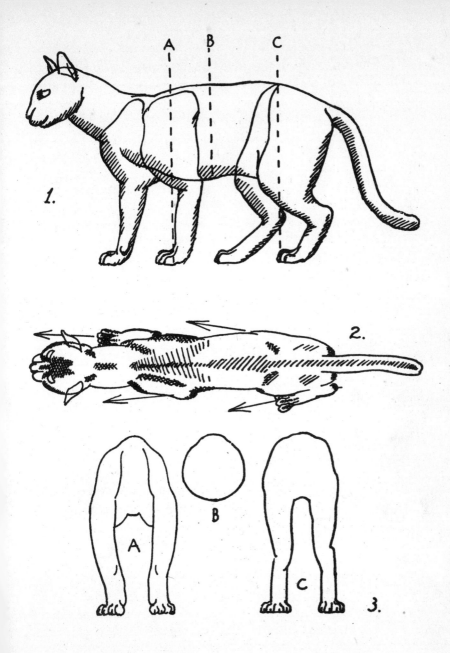

1.

2.

3.

CATS Diagram 4 is a figure expressing the peculiarities of bones of the domestic cat. The middle line on rib-cage marks the attachment of bones and cartilage. Except that the larger cats are heavier in their bones, these proportions would be true of the other species.

Attention is here drawn to the relative lengths of *humerus* and *ulna*.

The cheek and nose bones of skull are not so long as with the dog and there is a greater curve downwards to the canine teeth, which are proportionately longer. This formation is, probably, because of the cat feeding from animals smaller than itself; for in those larger cats the head is longer. Cause and effect might be argued as in the well-known chicken and egg conundrum.

LEOPARD Diagram 5 gives three figures of skulls of domestic cats, *A*, *B*, *C*, and *D*, that of a leopard. *B* is seen from above and is interesting on account of the projecting upper surfaces resembling those darker parts on head in Diagram 2: and again, in that the position of the rear part of lower jaw can be seen through the *orbit* holes (thus indicating complete shape of lower jaw).

The *zygoma* exerts great influence on the rounded outer and upper part of head, affecting form to the outer side just under the eye.

LION Diagram 6 shows front views of upper parts of skulls of lion
TIGER (*E*) and tiger (*F*). In *E* the nasal bone and the cheek bones are shown as being level, while *F* gives the noticeable difference in the skull of the tiger. Again, in that of the tiger, the canines will be seen as more curved and the diagram is *flatter*. This is because of the accustomed angle of the head—it is held more horizontally than that of the lion.

Diagram 7 gives the chief differences in the lower jaws of lion and tiger. The lion's is rounded downwards—it is rocking

56

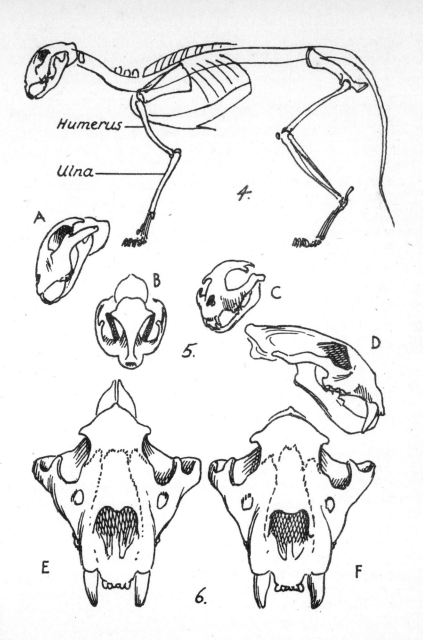

Humerus

Ulna

4.

A

B

C

5.

D

E

F

6.

or convex, whilst the tiger's is hollow or concave. Also, the posterior angle is slightly different, being more upright in the tiger.

In Diagram 8 will be seen plan of bony axes of cat: on the left, looking forwards, those attachments which are to the top; and on the right the underneath attachments. The *left* hinder foot is shown.

Relative projections of bones, in plan, will be noted from the dotted lines. The attitude of assembling is that seen in Diagram 5.

Curved, dotted lines show arcs of hand and foot facias.

For reference letters from front to rear read as follows:

for M.C., *Metacarpal* (hand bones).

for   S., *Scapula* (shoulder blade).

for   H., *Humerus* (arm bone).

for R.U., *Radius and Ulna* (lower arm bones).

for   P., *Patella* (knee cap).

for   F., *Femur* (thigh bone).

for   I.S., *Iliac Spine* (bone of hip).

for T.B., *Tibia and Fibula* (leg bones).

for   IM., *Ischium* (sitting bone).

for M.T., *Metatarsal* (foot bones).

for O.C., *Os calcis* (heel bone).

Diagram 9 gives vertical sections of several ribs. It will be noted that rib 13 springs from its attachment to backbone at a higher level than the lower numbers, and is at a *flatter* curve. The greatest curve is at about rib 8 and the lowest numbers are more upright.

The curved dotted line on left is descriptive of cartilaginous attachments to ribs from breastbone.

Diagram 10 shows bony axes of the limbs of a cat seen from

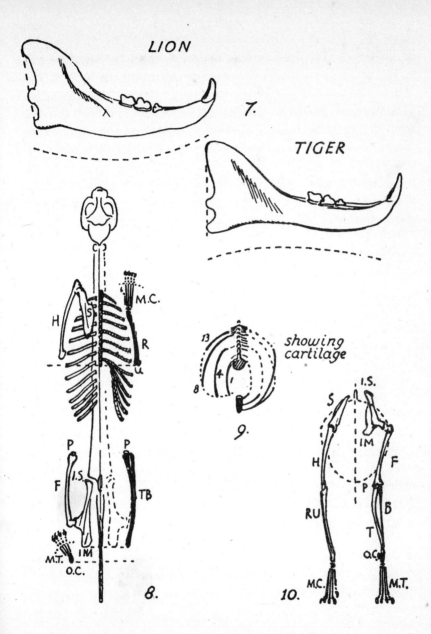

LION

7.

TIGER

M.C.

H   S

R

u

P   P

F   I.S.

TB

M.T.   IM

O.C.

8.

13

8   4

9.

showing
cartilage

I.S.

S

IM

H   F

P

RU   B

T

O.C.

M.C.   M.T.

10.

the front and reference letters as above will apply to this drawing.

In drawings of animals, the attitude is proportionately good in the degree to which it summarises an action. The attitude in suspension is never so satisfying as that proper to the completed action. It might be expressive enough should the moment for 'snapping' be chosen as immediately before the action is to take place. For example, the preparing-to-jump attitude is an expressive one. It is obvious that those most static attitudes will provide the most favourable ones to draw, though much can be done by the keen observer in line rhythm alone.

The *line of back* will be found of great expressional value in typifying the cat, especially when the animal is seen in profile.

The accompanying few diagrams will show some backs which are symbolic of different attitudes.

Diagrams 11 and 12 show the stealthy, creeping movements usual to a cat when stalking birds or mice.

Diagram 13 gives a typical example of a crouched cat lapping milk; while in Diagram 14 the cat is seen in greeting, with back already hollowed as if expectant of the caressing hand.

It would be well here to remember that one need not infer small knowledge from the slight drawing. Sufficiency in the drawing should be the aim of the draughtsman, and assuredly the purpose is achieved when sufficiency is attained. In these days of much talk of suitability to purpose, the draughtsman should be in no way behind the times.

Elimination of all but the essentials in an expressive drawing will denote power and not weakness. There is admission of incompetence in the statement 'it took me a week to draw this'. Efficient pride would proclaim 'I did it in three minutes'. It is

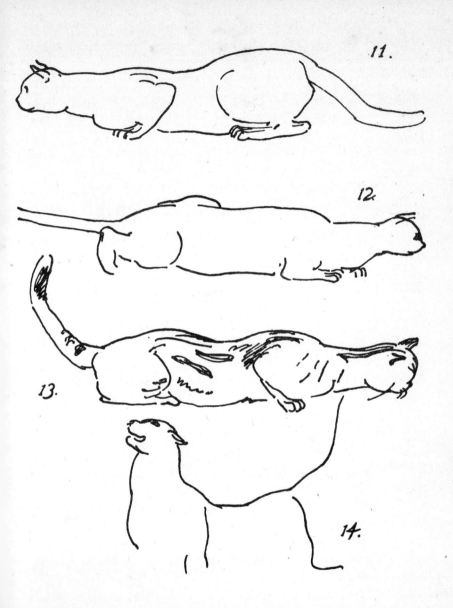

11.

12.

13.

14.

suggested though, that the student should spend much time thinking about and observing his subject.

Diagrams 15 to 18 are an attempt to show the approximations in hinders (outside and inside views) of cats to humans. It is clear that no scale is intended, but the cats could be of the small leopard kind.

Diagram 19, of a sleeping lioness, shows the hands and feet typical of the attitude and, whilst it is a very slight drawing, the under lines and opposing lines of top will be seen to be expressive of the ground line and the convex bones of framework respectively.

The cat's hairy covering does not show the cat any more than clothes can make the man, that is, anatomically. Do we not often see painted or even photographic likenesses of people whose sleeves, for instance, do not suggest that they contain arms? Without knowledge of the form one cannot render an adequate symbol of the form. The eye of the camera can only see, but the mind having understanding, one may by analytical study find a way to convey that which is more satisfying than an illusion.

Before examining the design of the coat it would be well to point to the difference, in the flesh covering, from that of the dog. These two animals are so ubiquitous that it should be possible for all to contrast them with little trouble. The cat seems to have more 'slack', or a kind of pendulous flesh, on the under and inside parts of him, which permits extreme movement in all limbs. This, and the attachments of limbs being freer (especially of shoulder and *humerus*, and *femoral* junction with *pelvis*), imparts a looseness or sinuosity to the movements which is remarkable of the kind. This 'slack' is increased in appearance by the hair *falling* more loosely on those parts and *laying* on the upper surfaces.

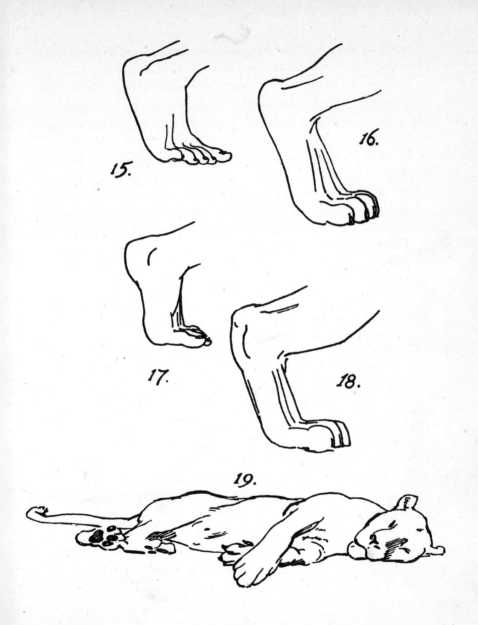

15.

16.

17.

18.

19.

On the shorter-haired domestic cat are several areas of quite short hair. The hair on these is inclined to stand upright and occurs on the undersides up to the first joints of legs, corresponding closely to the *plantar* and *palmar* surfaces; as well as on both lips, chin, ears, top of nose and, in some varieties, on top of head in front of and between the ears.

Diagram 20 shows these areas, marked by short strokes, and the general flow of the remaining hairy covering. The right side of diagram, looking forward, is of underneath view and the back and outsides are on the left. It will be observed that as well as the back seam there is the inferior seam, or that one on the under or belly side of the animal. A seam is also seen on each limb on the under side, posteriorly. Also two 'gussets' on the underside will be noticed, to accommodate the insetting of the limbs.

The radiation of hair, backwards and downwards on top, follows around the body to meet in the seam on the underside.

There is a group of hairy tufts to surround the ear and another tuft of radiating hair from within the ear.

In diagram, the curved lines *away* from head (top view) and *towards* head on insides of limbs are descriptive of the *lay* of the hair. It will be obvious that there are no such divisions on the cat, for this would result in a stepped appearance only made possible by artificial hairdressing.

This somewhat lengthy explanation of hair pattern will be found of inestimable value—the more one draws the animal the greater will be the assistance rendered by this knowledge.

Diagram 21, a side view, whilst showing the before-mentioned particulars of growth, suggests the ruff arrangement on throat and side of neck, to meet the downward-falling hair from top. This shows as a line behind ear in the radiation series and, to continue with the tailoring analogy, forms an outside pleat.

20.

Diagram 22 gives another side view, but this time the hair has bunched on elbows and knees to appear as radiations.

Attention is here drawn to the disengaged hair which is proper to an action where the underlying contours change. As will be seen, the line of back shows several sharp changes and with each change certain of the hairs separate. This is characteristic of fur and will be found of great importance to the draughtsman.

A 'kinked' tail (Diagram 23) would be easy to symbolise if this separation of hair at turns were remembered.

Diagram 24 shows hair directions at seams which call for an accent of a different kind from the remainder.

It must be understood that the drawing of the hair pattern in these diagrams is necessarily exaggerated. The *standing up*, the *bunching* and the *separation* of hair have all been made much of for diagrammatic purposes.

Attention must be drawn to one other 'texture'. It is that of the whiskers and eyebrows as also the side whiskers which become more noticeable on older animals. These are coarse in the cats, and in the larger cats, except for the black varieties, are white. The significance of their function is sufficiently indicated in a modern transatlantic slangism. So typical are they of the appearance of the animal, that on this count alone they must be noticed, though the animal would be incomplete and deprived of an essential natural faculty were he without them.

Diagram 25 gives a view which shows influence of ruff, chest seam and radiating tuft on knee of animal in the typical crouching attitude.

Diagram 26 shows break on top of head, with laying hair and standing-up hair reflecting light differently: the paler patches in front of ears showing the tufts transmitting light.

A black cat is seen in Diagram 27 and the fall and growth of

66

21.

22.

23.

24.

hair over the form are responsible for the distinctive pattern of darks. This diagram is inserted here as a check—a corrective to the opinion that interest in hair growth might lead to one 'losing the animal in the fur'.

TIGER   Diagram 28 is that of the head of a tiger and a few indications have been given of the growth of longer hair—to become a ruff on the older animal.

The vertical line drawn through the eye and corner of mouth will serve as a reminder that all the carnivorous animals have these two points in like relationship on the head and will show the tilt of skull in normal position.

The local colour markings proper to the tiger have been omitted and the symbol is descriptive of form alone. In conjunction with this last, the formation of skull is noticeably different from the next diagram.

LION   The lion's head seen in Diagram 29 is different in attitude and in implied bony under-structure. The growth of hair to make the mane is partly suggested and these two last diagrams conform to the comparative structural points noted earlier.

In both Diagrams 28 and 29 the lines of whisker roots are seen as contributing to the character and shaping of the animal's muzzles. There may be more rows, but others would be less well marked and the lines would be shorter.

One important piece of local colour is that hairless portion of lip which is exposed when the animal's mouth is opened. It is present in all carnivorous animals and whereas with the dog it shows more at the upper lip as he snarls, the formation of jaw and the peculiar manner of eating in the cat, exposes a greater proportion of the lower lip. This is opposite the back teeth and well back from the canines. It being dark in colour is noticeably characteristic in shape and is marked in Diagrams 28 and 29.

68

25.

26.

27.

28.

29.

Many of the cats are covered with stripes or spots which serve to camouflage the form, to terrify their victims, or make them indistinguishable in their natural surroundings.

There are two extreme systems—the marks *along* and the marks *down* the body.

Diagram 30 shows right half-plan of the system of marking on the common blotched or tabby cat. The important typical points are spaces on neck and behind, or on shoulder; a central back stripe with further back stripes just lower, and three stripes on each side; the middle ones being, usually, shorter than the others. The upper markings on legs are darted *towards* body, whilst the shoulder stripe is considerably branched and forms rings around the neck. The lower markings on legs (first joint) are *down* the joint.

TIGER   The tiger is typical of the other kind and Diagram 31 gives this system in brief. The shaded part represents the red-fawn portion of outside and back and the stripes are not to be regarded as of a thickness proportionate to the animal but indicative of system.

Darting of the limbs will be noticed and the neck space is shown.

The English wild cat, the fishing cats and several smaller varieties conform to this system.

The medium-sized cats seem to be marked with a combination of the two systems, for although the leopard, cheetah, jaguar, etc. have spots which can be divided into lines running along the body, they may be read as having the lines down the form as well. (For that matter all-over patterns are read diagonally also.)

SERVAL   The serval belongs to the longways system with unbroken lines at neck.

70

30.   31.

The *darts* of the insetting limbs will be obvious with all the cats.

The controlling system for markings on the head of the tiger will be seen in Diagram 32, front of head, and Diagram 33 is a development of Diagram 28. In this the local colour-markings have been added and are proved to be of structural significance. Also the black lip and white whiskers contribute much to the effect.

Diagram 34 gives an analysis of the side view of the whole animal and the downward stripes agree closely with the longways system.

Many of the stripes are in outline on the tiger and can be regarded as having imposed lighter eyes.

The local colour-markings are pigmentations on a lighter ground and the under sides of the cats are, as a rule, paler and often quite white.

A short list of chief differences follows in three divisions: the *base* is colour 'off white', the *stripes or spots* deal with the middle colour and *outlines* refer to the surrounds of spots or stripes as with leopard, ocelot, etc.

base:	stripes or spots:	outlines:
tiger, red-fawn,	black.	
leopard, fawn,	red-brown,	black rosette of small spots.
cheetah, pale fawn,	black.	
jaguar, grey,	grey to brown,	black, with dark brown centres to rosettes.
ocelot, grey,	brown,	dark brown.
puma, fawn,	brown.	
serval, grey to fawn,	dark brown to black.	
lynx, grey to fawn,	dark brown.	

32.

33.

34.

Local colour is seen to provide nearly all the essential accents in the few accompanying diagrams: 35 is of an ocelot in an attitude while eating, Diagram 36 is of a domestic kitten, and 37 is of a serval.

The example of domestic cat has stripes down the body and the two other examples have the stripes along the body.

In these three diagrams the base colour has been omitted.

Diagram 38 shows a clouded leopard, sneeringly antagonistic. The lower jaw, black lip, pale eye and white whiskers are typical, and though but slightly suggested, indicate combining factors of the peculiar feline kind.

The invariable pale eyes of cats are important features. With the exception of those of the cheetah, which is a daylight hunter, the eyes are capable of great dilation and this peculiarity imparts a visual character which seems in keeping with its unsociable and aloof nature.

It is said that the lion is the most gregarious of the cats and there is a calm about this creature which has, no doubt, earned him the reputation for nobility of temperament.

A strong draughtsman will wish to express something beyond pattern; he will try to convey the emotion of the animal, and keen observation will determine for him certain attitudes as symbolic of some emotion or other.

Attention should be drawn to the very expressive tail. This feature is as much alive as the remainder of the animal and will support, balance, comfort or lash him into a fury at will.

The ears not only hear but convey vindictive intentions. They hear forwards and outwards and the eyes *look forwards*.

The *sneer* of the lip is responsible for the whisker movement, and the whiskers are important features for expressing emotion.

35.

36.

37.

38.

Chapter 4

The Solid Horns: Deer, Giraffe

HORNED ANIMALS CAN BE DIVIDED INTO TWO CLASSES—THE
hollow horns and the solid horns.

This chapter will deal with the latter, though 'solid horn' is a
misnomer; for these are bony projections from the skull and,
excepting the reindeer, grow on the males only.

The number of tines or points in the branching increases as
the animal matures. The antlers are shed each year and take
from eight to nine months to grow to their fullest completion.
During this period blood is circulating in them and they are covered with a furry skin which falls away as the circulation is
stopped at base.

True deer differ considerably in size, markings and place of
origin. Most of them are very beautiful and they are distinguish-
able by their antlers and the divided toes—they walk upon the
third and fourth toes of each foot.

As with all the ruminate animals, the first toe is missing on
each foot and the outside ones (dewtoes) corresponding to the
human second and fifth, are but small and undeveloped.

The brain is smaller than with the carnivorous kinds and
there is a proportionate increase of the jaws lengthways.

They can be classed with the normal quadruped type, that is,
as having the length front of shoulder to *ischium* equal to height
of back at shoulder.

The kind is gregarious and associates in herds.

Deer inhabit localities where ground is hard, although the
divided hoof makes the foot an accommodating one and able, in

77

development, to support the animal on ice, in snow, forest, heath or rocky places.

Deer have the true grazing mouth and, whereas the horse tears in cropping, the deer kind cuts the green food closely, more in the manner of sheep and oxen.

Peculiarly a wild animal and a forest animal there is one species in domestication. This, the reindeer, is but the result of necessity, for it is cultivated in those latitudes where no other ruminant could survive.

Comparison of Diagram 1 of this chapter with that of the chapter on horses, will make clear the characteristic differences. The line of back does not show a hollow as with the horse, the top point of shoulder is more forward and the head is held more horizontally.

The neck attitude is somewhat similar to that of birds.

The legs, again, are slimmer: the animal is a toe walker, but any suspicion of precariousness in balance is negated by the spread of the toes, which in some varieties is considerable. One species, frequenting more marshy localities, walks partly on the pasterns. The pasterns correspond to the finger or toe bones in man.

Diagram 1 has the limbs drawn through to ground and the undercutting sides darkened to simulate the solid. The straight lines indicate proportions and the antlers have been omitted as these will be dealt with later.

Diagram 2 gives three sectional elevations at positions cut through as marked by dotted lines at *A, B, C* in Diagram 1. It will be seen that these differ from the horse in their relationships and shapes and both fore and hind quarters are slimmer.

Section *A* is taken through at about the ninth rib, where the animal is roundest. These two diagrams are a combination of the

78

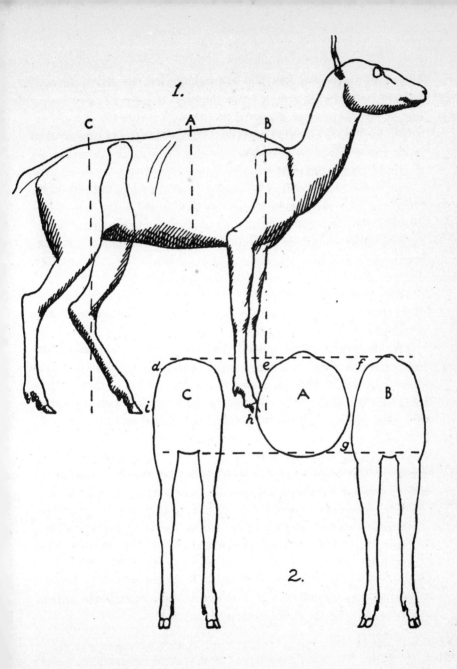

basic peculiarities of the deer kind and the separate species will
have characteristics which differ slightly, though never resembling the other groups closely.

The sectional elevations given in Diagram 2 are intended to
assist the student to discover how the form of the deer can be
divided into simple planes.

If the departure points on curves (marked by small letters on
Diagram 2) were marked on Diagram 1 and lines drawn between them, to connect at *ischium* and front of shoulder, the re-
sultant effect would be as Diagram 3. Examination of this diagram will show how the *drop* of the *pelvis* to rear and the more
upright shoulders are thus, roughly, symbolised.

Diagram 4 gives a three-quarter, front view of a deer, the forward contours (which are to be seen on right of Diagram 1) em-
phasised.

The antlers are of no special kind and undercutting and overhung parts have been shaded with vertical lines. The diagram
shows the antlers as projected from the protuberances above
eyes, and the eyes are at the *sides* of the head. This arrangement
of eyes is general in the non-predatory kinds of animals.

Students will not, generally, draw with confidence unless they
have acquired some other person's tricks. This is regrettable for,
although one might suppose that good manners or compliments
are expressed by this questionable habit, tricks of handling a
medium are more dangerous to a good tradition of drawing than
slang is to a spoken language. Far worse, for slang words become,
in time, part of a widely disseminated speech, whereas drawing
slang becomes meaningless in the proportion to which it is
specialised. It is imitable and makes one complacent to limited
knowledge and meagre power of expression. Most deplorable of
all, it prevents close examination of nature.

80

3.

4.

This digression leads to the axiom that *one having knowledge of the underlying structure will lose hesitation in describing the form graphically*.

A side elevation of the bony axes of a fallow deer is seen in Diagram 5. The dotted line, from *ischium* to underside of neck vertebræ, shows the bird-like balance of the neck. Note the great undercutting from *ischium* and behind *femur* to heel, and also the angle of shoulder with head of *humerus*. The inner curved line on rib-cage denotes attachments of cartilage.

Diagram 6 gives some sections of ribs: the right side of structure is shown and the numbers read from the front. It will be observed that a curved line has been drawn at top to mark the first turn downwards of ribs. The fifth *dorsal spinal process* is the highest in the column. Ribs, as far as the sixth, are very flat in section—giving the rib-cage a longer vertical than horizontal axis. The dotted lines show traces of cartilaginous attachments to breast-bone.

Diagram 7 shows rear view of right fore limb and shoulder. The projection of shoulder spine should be noted as also the curve of the *humerus*. The slight inward tendency of the *radius*, to brace the wrist inwards and backwards, and the casting outwards of the toes are points worthy of memorising. The curved, dotted line at top gives approximate axis and position of ninth rib as related.

In Diagram 8 will be seen a back view of the left hinder, with curve indicating the thirteenth rib in related projection. The tendency of the *femur* to turn inwards is a common anatomical feature. The heel bone projects towards the outer side and the composite mass of bones at this joint swells somewhat lower to the inside. The toes on the hinder do not turn outwards so noticeably, though in movement that attitude is usual.

82

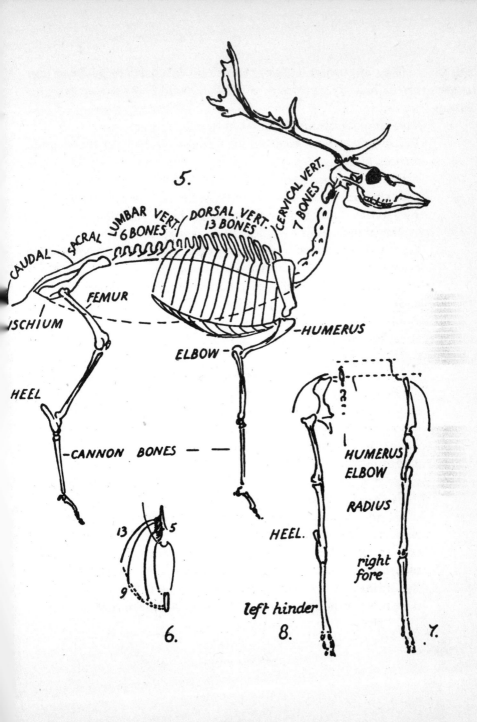

5.

CAUDAL

SACRAL

LUMBAR VERT. 6 BONES

DORSAL VERT. 13 BONES

CERVICAL VERT. 7 BONES

FEMUR

ISCHIUM

HUMERUS

ELBOW

HEEL

CANNON BONES

13

5

9

6.

HEEL.

left hinder

8.

HUMERUS

ELBOW

RADIUS

right fore

7.

Diagram 9 shows plan of bony axes of a male fallow deer. On the right are upper part of skull; shoulder blade and trace of *humerus*; the top side of rib-cage and *pelvis*; position of *trochanter of femur* and knee.

The left side of diagram carries one antler and the dotted, curved line gives position points of greatest projection from skull.

The right half shows *orbit* with its forward and outward direction and the attachment of antler on brow, and the left shows the lower jaw projecting less from centre than the upper one.

Ribs tend to curve backwards and downwards as they increase in number, and the dotted line shows the points where they commence their downward inclination. The foremost ribs are blade-like—facilitating movement of, and supporting shoulder blades.

The transverse spines in the *lumbar vertebræ* point forward and the front *iliac spine* follows this direction.

The *pelvis* is narrow and the *ischium* projects a lot to the rear.

The trace of the *femur* converges *inwards* whilst the *tibia* descends *outwards* and backwards.

Forwards, the lower inside-to-rib-cage is seen and the inner curved line shows attachments to cartilage. Note that the inner part of ellipse of the first set of ribs is more to the front than where it is attached to backbone. This is responsible for a characteristic piece of surface form.

Diagram 10, a side elevation of skull and antler of fallow deer, shows how the arch of cheek bone and *zygoma* support the antlers. The continuous line at top shows centre line of skull and the broken line of second curve gives the inner buttress to *orbit*. The *orbit*, also, is drawn with a dotted line at top showing how these two overlaying curves change the outline of skull.

84

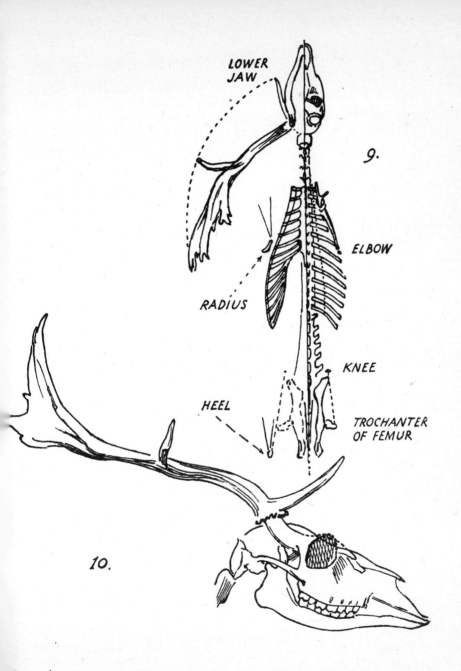

LOWER JAW

9.

ELBOW

RADIUS

KNEE

HEEL

TROCHANTER OF FEMUR

10.

The sharp teeth at muzzle end of lower jaw radiate forwards (as suggested in Diagram 11) to cut the grass against the pad on upper *maxillary*.

Diagram 11 shows the nasal bone inserted between the inner buttresses of orbits, and a front elevation of antler.

Diagram 12 is an attempt to provide a constructional guide to the proper balancing of the antlers.

It refers to the fallow deer, and the 'saucer' (the surrounding form to antlers) is a means of maintaining the hollows as well as providing extreme points of *tines*. A *tine* is a projection from the main beam of the antler and may have *snags* or lesser projections. To one versed in woodcraft, the age of an animal may be ascertained on counting the tines and snags.

Some deer have the 'saucer' much shallower than others, which may be more elliptical. Some 'saucers' are more upright. Again, some antlers are more circular in section, while some kinds of deer have what are called palmated antlers.

The palmate antler is as though a webbing had been stretched between the tines and snags and then ossified; and usually occurs, as with the fallow deer, more on the rear tines. This is a useful description, for the veins occurring on the palmated parts coincide with the points and join to the main *beam* of the antler.

Either by modifying these proportions or exaggerating the projections given in Diagrams 5-12 almost any deer type may be drawn with assurance.

Being denisons of the forest, deer are provided with antlers both as protective disguise (antlers resemble tree branches very closely) and defensive weapons, for attack would, more often than not, come from above and the enemy might be entangled as a prelude to being crushed.

11.

12.

Antlers differ in design according to the kind of deer upon which they grow. The skin which encases the antlers during the early months before maturity is furry. This takes light curiously, appearing as a velvety sheath, and makes the antlers seem softer and *fatter* than they will be finally.

Some 'saucers' are given, in the accompanying diagrams, which will permit easy recognition of the different kinds. The upper series shows plans and the lower one gives tilts and elevations of the same. Thus, 13 and 17 apply to the one species and the positions of diagrams indicate their relationships. Individual members will vary, but the system is maintained in all of the one species.

Diagrams 13 and 17 show plan and 'saucer' of the caribou and reindeer system. It will be noticed that the 'saucer' is deep and resembles a basin. Except that the caribou often has more palmated antlers than the reindeer the plan and elevation will stand for both. One brow tine is invariably more elongated than the other in these kinds. The 'saucer' is not very circular in plan and the beam, or main stem, of the antler is elliptical.

Diagrams 14 and 18 give growth of elk or moose antlers. These are heavy, much palmated and the beam at base is circular in section.

The wapiti system of antler is seen in Diagrams 15 and 19. The 'saucer' is wide though shallow, and the beam is cylindrical; but the tines are more elliptical in section. There is a brow tine and the fourth tine is heavy and larger than the others.

Red deer have a narrower and more shallow system than the last.

Diagrams 16 and 20 show system of sambur and is common to many American and Asiatic kinds.

Diagram 21, a side view, gives lines on body to show factitious

88

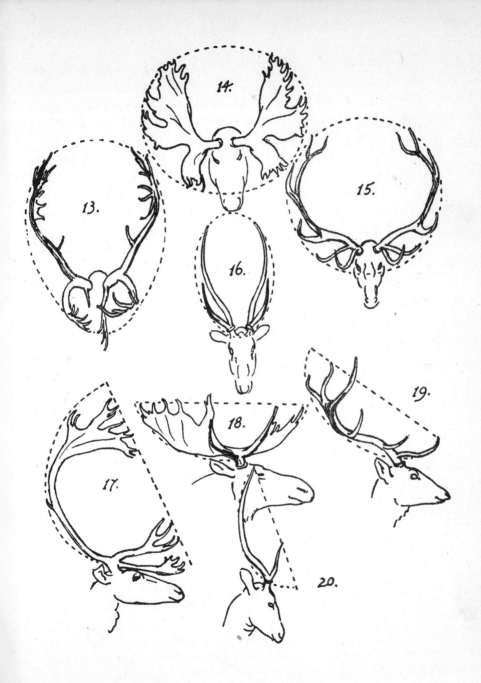

planes; and the continuous line, drawn from front of *pelvis* downwards to hock, is one which, end on, could be tested with a straight-edge and found to vary but slightly from the straight or right line.

The animal is governed by this in his attitude when resting on the ground, and Diagram 22 shows the three sections (as given in Diagram 2 of this chapter) when in the position indicated. The section of fore quarters will remain upright and the barrel, being rather flat underneath, does not change. The flatness of the surface of hind quarters given in 21 engages with ground and the typical resting attitude is adopted. Note the turn of back line and the dropped tail.

Diagram 23 is from an animal in the position mentioned and the action will be clear.

Presumably, the action of kneeling with the forelegs before settling the quarters, is due to this accommodating flatness of hind quarters and the said accommodation arranged as being the means of presenting the antlers more readily when arising (for the deer kind lift the hind quarters first when striking camp).

A word here as to grouping. It would be wise, when composing animals of the deer kind, to group them as subject to some common impulse. The timidity of the hinds would be expressed by their communal feeding no less than their headlong flight and, although the fearless note of the buck is opposed to the nervous agitation of the remainder of the herd, his attitude should emphasise the general hesitancy.

Above all it should be remembered that one animal or a portion done beautifully will not compensate for lack of cohesion in the group.

Diagram 24 is of a female roe deer in an attitude while negotiating a bank. The head, neck and shoulder thrust forward,

90

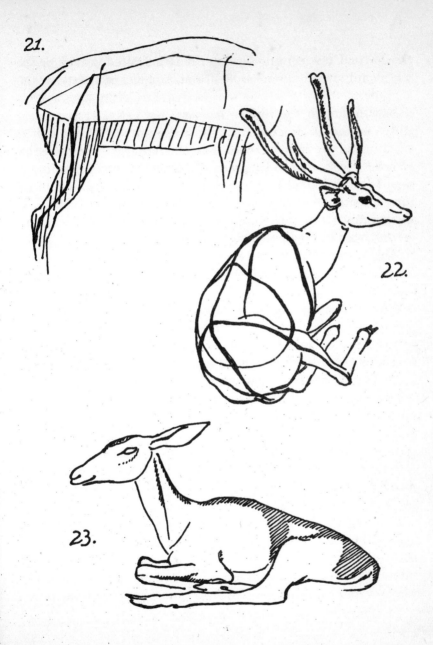

21.

22.

23.

the lines of projecting rib-cage, the stern raised, although the tail is still curled downwards, are all significant points in the attitude.

Now although the hinder legs are, normally, braced fairly stiffly, any disturbing noise will cause the animal to bend all legs slightly and the hinders more than the fore legs. The direction of bend is indicated in Diagram 25 where the top of shoulder is seen as much higher than the rear end of the animal. A further sign of agitation is displayed by the pricked, distended ears and dilated nostrils of this young roe buck, who is poised ready to spring away at any further sign of disturbance.

This is the early season of the year and the animal is yet in 'velvet'. This term is used when the young nobs are in the early stages of their development. Later in the year, when the antler is fully formed, the 'velvet' falls away.

Excuse will be made for the introduction of a giraffe because of his 'solid horns'. Also, this animal walks on the third and fourth toes in the way peculiar to deer and he is a true ruminant.

Diagram 26 shows a galloping giraffe: the *back line* and the curious formation of the fore quarters and length of neck will be noted as being typical. It seems almost as though the animal propels the hinders forward in this action, using the forks of fore quarters somewhat like an inverted catapult fork.

The great height of the withers, and stilt-like attitude in walking, give the particular character in all actions of this animal.

The diagrams on the opposite page are not to scale.

It will be remarked that 'anatomy' in this treatise deals with bones and that, apart from a few comparisons with kinds other than the animals under review, functions and features of muscles are negated.

24.

25.

26.

From the draughtsman's point of view, by far the most important part of the structure is bony. This has been proved in all the chapters by the axes of limbs determining their directions or weights; and it must be axiomatic that the proportions of rib-cage and *pelvis* are responsible for carriage or gait. An illustration of the importance of draughtsmen being acquainted with bones will be seen in Diagrams 27-29.

Diagram 27 shows a side elevation of skull of giraffe: the dotted lines, downwards, give some idea of the projections and hollows.

In the live animal, almost the whole is subcutaneous and might be covered by flesh to look rather like Diagram 28. In this diagram the upper *maxillary* and teeth are shown to affect contour and the influence of *zygoma* and lower border of *orbit* is very great. The curious prehensile upper lip, and its pendulous appearance as it surrounds the upper pad of the true ruminant, is a feature of great interest in this animal. The eyes are placed at the sides of the head and the long sweeping eyelashes are of great textural importance as also is the upright mane which descends the nape of neck onto withers.

If one were to view the animal from a three-quarter back position and from rather below, the projections from the draughtsman's point of view might be contained within the stronger dotted line seen in Diagram 27, which is drawn from horn to *pre-maxillary*. Diagram 29 gives this point of view and all the salient features of bone will be recognised.

The texture of hair will affect the appearance in many ways. It might, in its simplest form, be tufted to alter a contour; but there is a more subtle change effected by the various *directions* of growth.

94

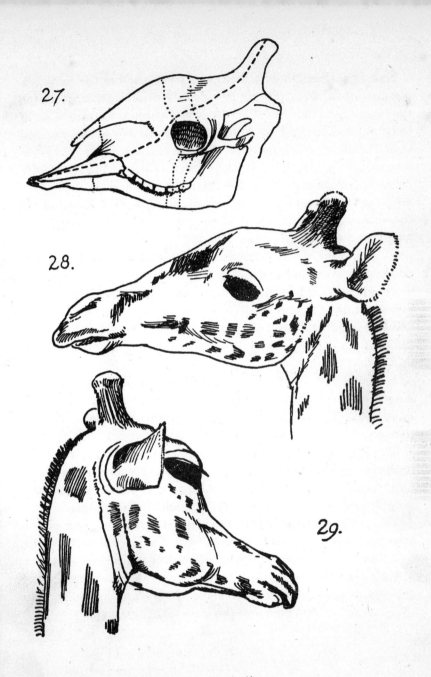

27.

28.

29.

Should a contour be covered evenly with hair of equal length, but in two directions, these two directions of growth will be lit differently under most conditions. For example, suppose that the light *rakes along* one system it would *drop into* the other. The light would be reflected from the one and the other would absorb the rays. When it is remembered that, according to background, one or other of these intervals or values will be more emergent it remains to note these differences with exactitude in the drawing. The inside surface will require analysing—not alone for the moments when the surface is contained within the outline, but for when it should in turn become outline—on the draughtsman assuming a different view.

DEER

Diagram 30 shows hair arrangement on chest of sambur deer and is peculiar to this kind. The radiating portions on legs and again to centre of breast are of softish, rather long hair.

Diagrams 31 and 32 give development of this pattern when lit, in 31 from the left, and 32 gives the opposite effect of lighting.

A Manchurian sica deer is diagrammatised in 33 and the longer lines on front of shoulders and legs show the 'flow' of short hair. The individuals of each species will be similar though the species differ widely in their hair arrangements.

Ears, eyes and noses deserve particular attention for they vary in textures. The ear, playing a large part in expressional drawing, should be clearly defined in its several parts, and the hair growth proper to kind or position symbolised accordingly.

The chief remarkable points of pricked ears of sica deer will be seen in Diagram 34, as from the front. The shaded parts on the leaf are bare, and tufted lines appear on the main veins.

Diagrams 35 and 36 show hair arrangement on ears of Eastern red deer and fallow deer respectively. The fallow ear has shortish hair on the back and the lines give direction.

96

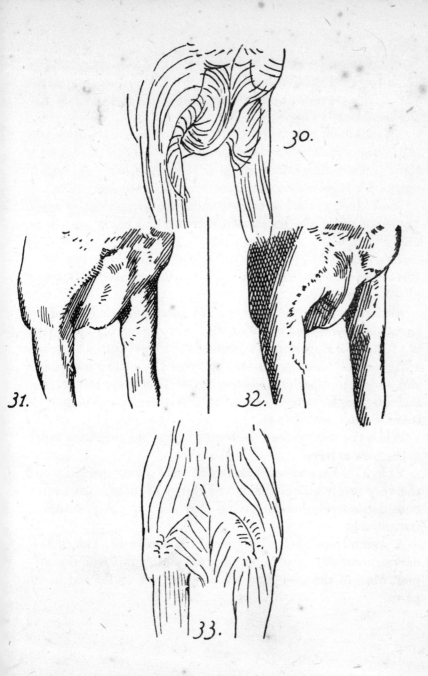

30.

31.

32.

33.

A three-quarter end view of ear is given of Eastern red deer in Diagram 37. The tube is hair-covered and the shell and leaf are bare. (The parts are named here to describe the obvious divisions and need no explanation.)

Arrangement of hair on the face of a fallow deer will be seen in Diagram 38. The dark part on top of nose shows hair which is short and standing rather upright. The fallow has a wet nose— hair does not grow around the nostrils or in front down to lip.

Some kinds, as the elk, caribou and reindeer, have hairy noses; the small triangular bare patch between and below nostrils on moose is peculiar.

The *lachrimatory gland* (below eye) when very marked is surrounded by radiating hair, somewhat as indicated in Diagram 39—Eastern red deer.

Antlers, both for kind and texture, should be studied and the particular corrugated radiation on the crowns at base of antlers is a feature of importance, as well as the longer tufted and radiating hair surrounding these. Each year the antlers increase in size and in number of tines and snags. This up to the years of maturity, eight to ten years, after that there is a tendency for them to deteriorate in size.

When the skin dries off the horns it splits in a manner likened to the bark of trees.

'Colour' is here meant to relate to local colour markings and the very lovely and distinctive markings of some kinds contribute decoratively besides giving conviction to the attitudes of the animals.

A sketch from a wapiti is given in Diagram 40. The curious darker undersides give an air of great pigmentation to this animal. Most of the deer kind are paler on the under and inside parts.

98

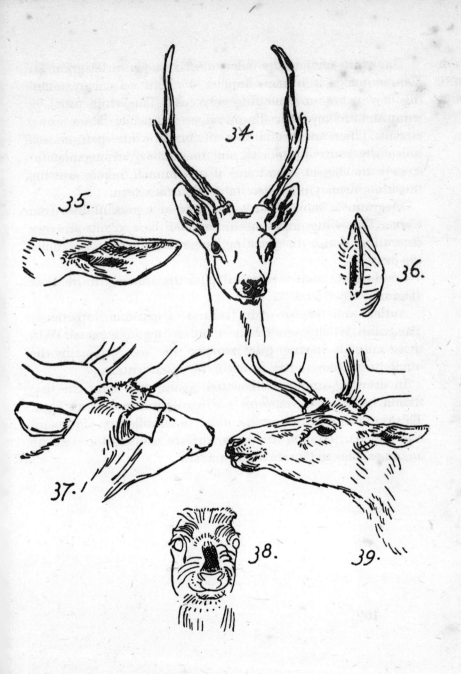

34.

35.

36.

37.

38.

39.

The white circle of the fallow deer is shown in Diagram 41. This animal is, as its name implies, of a light red colour, softening downwards to something very pale. The white patch on rump and the top centre line of tail are defined by darker brown accents. There are several lines of circular white spots on each side of the centre line of back, and their orderly arrangement increases the elegant appearance of this animal, besides assisting the draughtsman in his description of surface form.

Diagram 42 shows the colour pattern of a graceful deer from China. The white flecks and the smaller dark accents are very decorative. Notice the radiating longer hair on chest and under the belly.

Local colour alone is responsible for the drawing in the three diagrams, 40, 41 and 42.

Antlers and feet are both features of extreme importance. The polish, ribbing and colour of antlers should be noted. With those animals having pale *pasterns* the toes, especially the hinder toes, show as dark points in the colour pattern.

In drawing animals silhouetted against the light, the hair should be noted as more or less regularly transmitting light. This is most noticeable on the under and inside parts of the animal, for hair 'lays' on the upper surfaces and tends to separate on under sides and inside limbs and tail.

40.

41.

42.

Chapter 5

Horses, Zebra, Donkey

THE HORSE IS PECULIARLY CONSTRUCTED FOR SPEED AND endurance. It is amenable to training, and in this, perhaps, lies the reason for its present physical character. This animal as we know him is the result of breeding during countless generations of mankind. The powerful shire or cart horse differs considerably from the thoroughbred or race horse. Use has adapted structure and trained capabilities, in these two varieties, proper to their several functions.

This chapter will deal with the typical horse form: the zebra, kiang, mule, ass and donkey have characteristic features in common with the horse.

The length of head and neck and the greater width of hind quarters, together with the enlarged development of the single *cannon bone*, separate the horse type from other quadrupeds.

The peculiar horse form is one of great beauty and is specially suited to localities where ground is firm and dry. The hoof or nail covering to the developed middle toe is the natural consequence of the animal's living in those regions; and members of the family which, as the ass, live in more rocky or stony localities have (in common with other kinds of animals in those localities) more upright toes. The hoofs in these cases are more capable of withstanding the shock of impact, that is, of dispelling in part the vibration before it is transmitted to the delicate organism of the animal through the softer pad of the foot. The soft pad of the under side of the foot is known as the frog. Where the horse is bred in softer districts, such as meadow land, the hoof becomes longer and flatter, to project forwards.

Diagram 1 gives the mean proportions of the horse.

Diagram 2, the cart horse, is heavier and, as with all heavy animals, the shoulder is more vertical than this feature appears in Diagram 1.

The *withers*, or that portion of back between and just behind shoulders, will appear as higher with the thoroughbred (Diagram 3).

The length of head and angle at which it is held follow the shoulder pretty closely on the same animal.

In these three diagrams, the undercutting lines have been darkened to give relief from the paper—to give a semblance of solidity. Though it is not pretended that the projections are adequately symbolised, the darks will be found to round the masses in their relationships.

Perusal of the dotted lines will make clear some of the most remarkable differences in the proportions of the three types of domesticated horse.

The differences observed in the lines drawn from noses to ends of tails, in the three figures, will point once again the importance of commencing one's studies with this statement, either for type or action.

Now, however faithful one's notation of incident on the edge, the outline of a thing will be as flat as the paper on which it is drawn. And though many diagrams of the same thing, seen from different view points, will serve to establish proof of one's study, yet, in the same way that architects find a perspective projection to be of superlative value, so a symbol for the foreshortening and projecting of masses or incidents will be of great pictorial value to the freehand draughtsman of animals. This

104

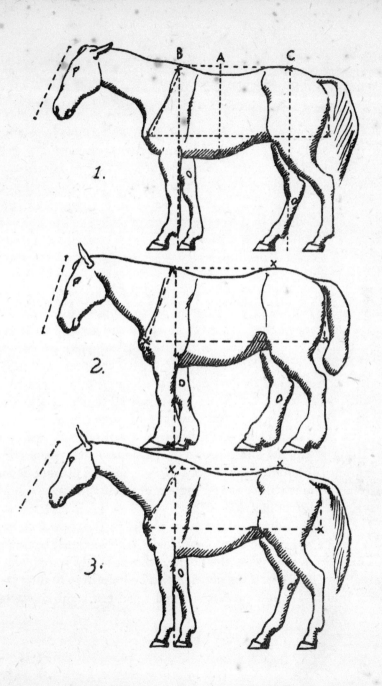

symbol will not be possible unless one understands the whole in relationship to the sub-divisions, or the smaller incident as being the result of anatomical structure or of some action of the parts.

Diagram 4 gives vertical sections of barrel, withers to ground and quarters to ground: these shown as cut through at *A*, *B* and *C* in Diagram 1, and the outlines of *B* and *C* are indicative of the surface projections. *D* shows the section of neck insertion.

It will be found advisable to practise *abstracting* from the complex horse form in the earlier stages of study; and to this end Diagram 5 shows straight lines drawn from positions of salient points of sectional contours calculated on side view diagram. The two tones imposed indicate the lesser illumined parts (*i.e.* those portions not turned upwards) and the undercutting darkest portion. Note that the paler tone was applied first and the darker tone added. This is a method which will give, in studying from live animals, the greatest number of complete drawings; for if one has only time to add one tone to the line, it is sufficiently expressive of form. Further time spent on the drawing should permit more truths or additional statements; and the drawing should only need additions and not alterations.

It has been stated that an outline conveys only a flat figure. A flat thing is a plane and has two dimensions. A convex or concave thing, although a continuous surface, is not a plane; but for facile notation it will be found convenient to invent what might be styled *factitious planes*.

The lines bounding the factitious planes in Diagram 5 do not exist on the animal as plane boundaries (the sectional contours in Diagram 4 show that the surface continuously rounds outwards); nevertheless, some division will be helpful in finding the mean line of greatest projection; and upon the right choice of

106

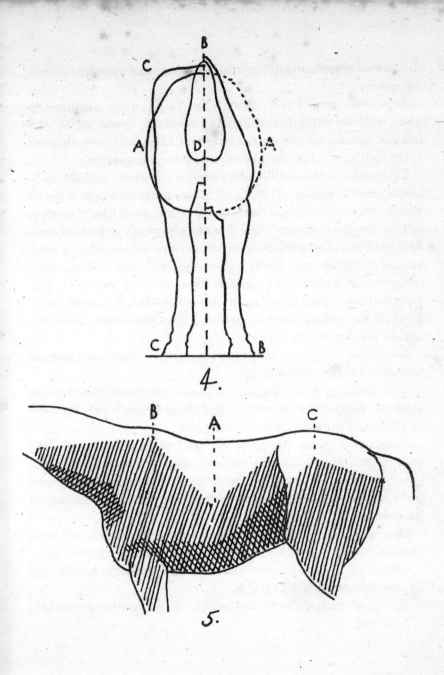

4.

5.

this line of departure will rest the success of one's personal drawing symbol.

In a well-conditioned animal the flanks, from shoulder to knee, will be without considerable contours. Some ponies and heavier breeds, also older or overfed animals, will have the barrel projecting outside the line of shoulders and quarters.

Diagram 6 is the outline of a horse in elevation; and the horizontal lines shown at *A, B, C, D, E* are taken through at levels which show the various features of contours at their greatest differences. For instance, line *D*, taken through at level of *ischium*, gives greatest projection of barrel; and the insertion of neck at base is higher than lower end of shoulder (and consequently the greatest projection of shoulder has not been reached). The horizontal sectional contours at this level—line *D*—sufficiently describe the surface incident, which differs remarkably from the higher set of contours of line *E*.

Diagrams 7 -11 show plan sections at levels *A* to *E*, and dotted lines give relative projections.

Commencing with Diagram 7, it will be noticed that the toes point outwards from centre and that those of the hinder feet are more turned outwards than the fore pair.

Diagram 8 gives the plan sections, at two levels, of *hock* or heel and the wrist; the curved, dotted line indicates the curve, in plan, of fascia of wrist, turned outwards as the toe: the heel bone is rather more to the outer side than central at that level.

Diagram 9 shows plan sections at knee and elbow level; note that the longer axes of sections are forward and turn outwards.

Diagrams 10 and 11 give plan contours at levels marked by lines taken through at *D* and *E*.

The combining of the vertical section with these horizontal sec-

108

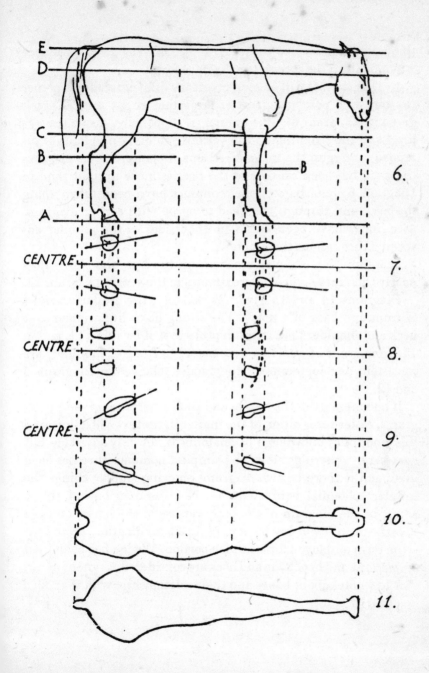

E

D

C

B —————— B

6.

A

CENTRE

7.

CENTRE

8.

CENTRE

9.

10.

11.

tions should provide a basket structure of very great assistance when plaiting the intervening surface form.

In Diagram 12 will be seen boundary lines of factitious planes (to join with points of greatest projection at the several levels given in Diagram 6). The animal is, supposedly, above the eye level and the hatching on the various sub-dividing planes is intended to suggest the mean directions of planes. In this diagram the head has been raised and the neck is more upright than in Diagram 6, but the sectional contours have been taken along the neck and through the head to agree with earlier diagram. Also, tones have been added to undersides in the manner advocated throughout these notes.

Diagram 13 is a development from the last, and shows how nearly this freer symbol approximates to the severe Diagram 12.

Diagrams 14 and 15 give, respectively, three-quarter views of front and back of a horse. The strong black lines, taken over neck and shoulder to maximum projection of barrel in 14, and in 15, from front of quarters over barrel to front of shoulder, are consistent developments of the practice followed in Diagrams 5 and 12.

If one memorises the names and their references given in diagrams, easier recognition of the matter in the text will follow, and this amount of knowledge of anatomy is not only advisable but necessary. Where possible, the simplest nomenclature has been used, and if there be two diagrams showing similar things the simpler colloquial equivalent has been used in one of them. Thus, in the diagram of the bony carcase of the horse, on page 113, the term *femur* has been used. In a later diagram, *thigh bone* is the term employed for a similar portion. Wedge has been used for *phalanx* and heel bone and hock are considered as synonymous.

A few notes about bones and their relationships will, if applied

12.

13.

14.

15.

to one's own practice, help to give to one's drawing the spring, stiffness and support which the armature affords in the modeller's work. In fact, the bones achieve all that the armature does, as well as giving protection to many internal organs of the animal's anatomy.

Diagram 16 gives the bony axes of a thoroughbred horse; one side of limbs and head showing.

The relative vertical and horizontal relationships will be noted as giving greater fluency in drawing from the animal. The continuous line of back should be observed, as also the very great projection of spines on the *dorsal vertebræ*; again, the greatest projection of rib barrel (at junction of false ribs with cartilage) must be memorised.

Diagrams 17 and 19 give hypothetical views of the outer border of human left arm and leg. An attempt has been made to foresee the consequent attitude of these if all the bones of hand and foot were removed, excepting only those to which attaches the central digit in each. These bones, enlarged because of their more considerable service, are, in the animal, called the *cannon bones*.

Diagrams 18 and 20 show similar views of corresponding limbs of a horse. The dotted, curved lines show axial curves at centres of limbs to ground. The similarities are obvious and further investigation of the horse will undoubtedly afford many other points of resemblance.

The lettered straight lines show corresponding measurements on the two limbs: thus *A-A* gives length from top of *ulna* to base of *radius* (one bone really in the horse) and from articulating upper end of *tibia* to top of *meta tarsal* (or foot bone) as being equal. Equivalent comparisons will be seen at *B-B* and *C-C* in the same diagrams.

112

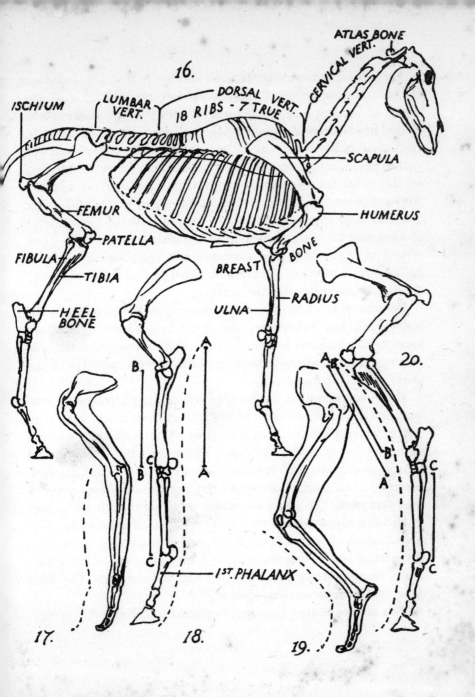

16.

ATLAS BONE

CERVICAL VERT.

ISCHIUM

LUMBAR VERT.

DORSAL VERT.
18 RIBS - 7 TRUE

SCAPULA

FEMUR

HUMERUS

PATELLA

FIBULA

TIBIA

BREAST BONE

RADIUS

HEEL BONE

ULNA

20.

A

B

B

A

A B

B

A

C

C

C

C

B

C

1ST PHALANX

17.

18.

19.

Diagram 21 shows side elevation of the skull of a shire horse. This, as will be seen, is appreciably heavier than that of the thoroughbred or that of the general utility horse. The curved, dotted line takes in the foremost projection of cheek bone (which, continued posteriorly, makes the inferior or lower border of eye socket and, finally, becomes the *zygoma*), the forward rounding of the nasal bone (common to most types of horses) and the greatest projection of lower jaw. These three points will aid in proportioning the head.

Diagram 22 is developed from the earlier one of the bony structure, and shows the subcutaneous bone (as that part is called which is not so deeply embedded in flesh and which influences more noticeably the surface).

Obviously, the number of ribs showing will depend upon the individual, but otherwise, the chief remarkable points are shown. The darker areas show the osseous influence on the side of the animal and those thicker outlines are expressive of the same on the silhouette.

If one supposes that bones serve two prime purposes—to support and to protect—the grouping into the two kinds so serving will be an easy matter. It will be clear that the rib-cage is of the domed order, as is also the skull. These two chambers, vaulted within and buttressed without, are admirably suited to their purposes. The flying buttress of the *zygoma* and the curves of all parts make for great resistance and might well have suggested to early architects the utility of the arch in building. The *pelvis*, again, comes within this division of protecting bones. The division of supporting bones would be comprised of the backbone, not forgetting the neck portion, and the legs. The arch form will be apparent throughout.

The curved dotted line in Diagram 23 includes the several

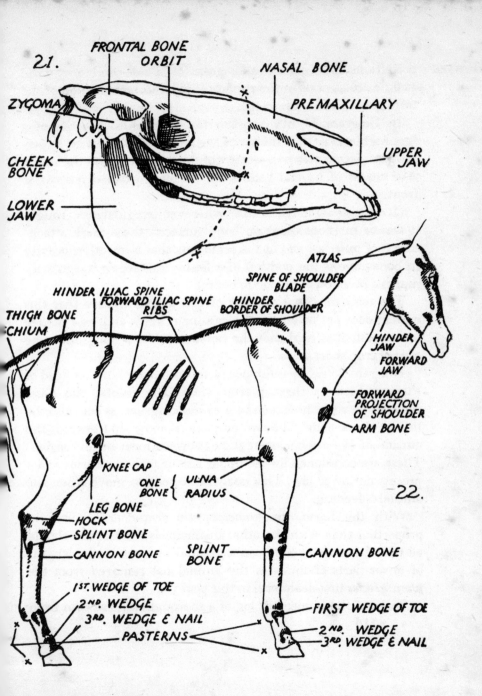

21.

FRONTAL BONE
ORBIT
NASAL BONE
ZYGOMA
PREMAXILLARY
CHEEK
BONE
UPPER
JAW
LOWER
JAW

ATLAS
SPINE OF SHOULDER
BLADE
HINDER ILIAC SPINE
FORWARD ILIAC SPINE
RIBS
HINDER
BORDER OF SHOULDER
THIGH BONE
ISCHIUM
HINDER
JAW
FORWARD
JAW
FORWARD
PROJECTION
OF SHOULDER
ARM BONE

KNEE CAP
ONE
BONE {
ULNA
RADIUS
22.
LEG BONE
HOCK
SPLINT BONE
CANNON BONE
SPLINT
BONE
CANNON BONE

1ST. WEDGE OF TOE
2ND. WEDGE
3RD. WEDGE & NAIL
PASTERNS
FIRST WEDGE OF TOE
2ND. WEDGE
3RD. WEDGE & NAIL

projections noted earlier in Diagram 21. Those combined in the outline are obvious in their relationship, but introduction of the third gives form to the shape.

In Diagram 24 will be seen the subcutaneous bones of a thoroughbred as they influence the frontal surface. The arrowhead on *premaxillary* is worthy of note, for it shows the upper attachment of lip and defines the division between nostrils at front.

(It is a general truth that wherever irregularities, roughnesses or incisions occur on bony surfaces, these mark attachments of muscles; and in the same way that a smooth concavity in bones marks the position of a fleshy muscle, an irregularity marks a junction of tendon to bone.)

The teeth in the upper jaw of this diagram prove that this animal does not belong to the ruminant kinds and, as a matter of interest, it is held that the horse requires a 'long bite'—he cannot crop short grass.

Diagram 25 shows influence of subcutaneous bone on head of thoroughbred—a three-quarter view. The frontal and nasal areas agree with those seen in previous diagram, as does also the line of cheek bone. The two projections above and towards the outside of eye are characteristic of surface form in this region. These are occasioned by the upper rim or process of orbit and a process on lower jaw. This last will be seen to move when the animal is feeding.

With the horse, the *humerus* and *femur* are shorter in proportion than with the other quadrupeds; and notice should be taken that there has been a gradual increase in the lengths of lower parts of limbs as the animal has removed from the *plantigrades* first dealt with in this book.

Bones of the hinder left leg of a thoroughbred are seen from

116

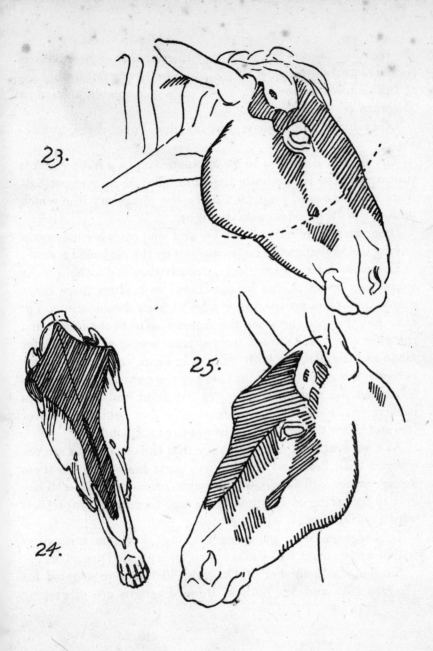

23.

24.

25.

the rear in Diagram 26. Note that the *os calcis* or heel bone is more towards the outside; this diagram being of a left limb.

Influence of nearer surface and edge will be seen applied in Diagram 27.

Diagrams 28 and 29 show similar action, but of the right fore-leg.

The darkened portion in 28 approximates to a hollow and it summarises the whole limb: the limb being at its greatest outward and backward projection down the imaginary line which bounds the darkened area on the right.

Diagram 29 is of a right fore-leg and seen from behind; again having the subcutaneous bones marked by the darkened areas.

Domes, considered interiorly, are cavities, and although the supporting bones cannot be considered as cavities there occur many concavities on the inner sides of bony combinations. For example, the space between the anterior spine of the *iliacus* and the knee cap, that between the posterior border of the shoulder blade and the *ulna* are both concave in form. Again, the hollow between the greatest upward curve of the *cervical* group of *vertebræ* and the elongated spines at the front end of the *dorsal* backbones is a discrepancy as marked as that behind the lower jaw and below the first four or five of the neck bones.

As a general rule, one might say that the convexities are not covered with flesh and the concave parts hold flesh. To these fleshy masses will be given the name *articulate masses*. They give to the spring of the underlying arch form that compactness which is so noticeable with the horse.

In Diagram 30, a galloping thoroughbred, the concavities will be apparent, as will also the arch form alluded to earlier.

Similar action to that of Diagram 30 has been adopted for Diagrams 31 and 32. Both of these diagrams are of grazing

118

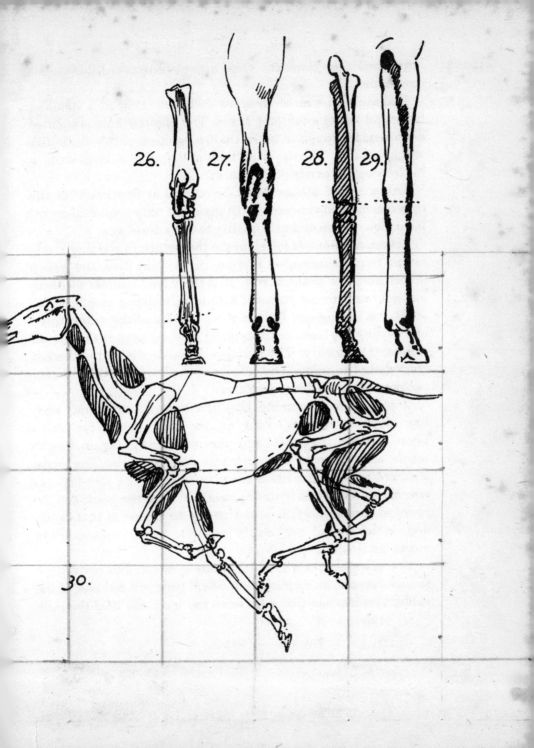

26. 27. 28. 29.

30.

horses and they show the chief articulate masses fitted to the concavities.

Diagrams 33 and 34 show an underside view of a standing horse and one of a jumping horse. The lines are both simplified and carried through in order that recognition of the continuity will be assured. The upper portions of both sets of limbs show as buttressing the cavity of the thorax.

The action of a horse must be studied at first hand; or the conventionalised rendering will give, not only second-hand information, but second-rate quality to one's drawings.

Action, as intended here, means that which in walking is different from cantering—different in the way that the gallop differs from the artificial trot. It is the whole manner of doing and not one arrested attitude. A human, walking, might be described as having one foot on the ground and the other raised and passing the first. But this could be done even if the person remained stationary. The business of walking is quite different from that of running. The balance of the body and the separate positions of all the limbs are altered

It is well to remember that the horse is a runner and, like all true runners, runs on his toes. These are more often directed forwards and downwards and again, backwards and upwards than upwards and forwards. The horse does not easily bring his hinders in front of the fore-legs (as was shown with the running dog). Whilst the back can be rounded considerably, it is not nearly so supple as that of the dog, which in all probability accounts for the restriction of action last mentioned.

The draughtsman's job is to create symbols, and correctness should never be an impediment. Much time will be saved if the student remembers that a horse on the level will hold the neck

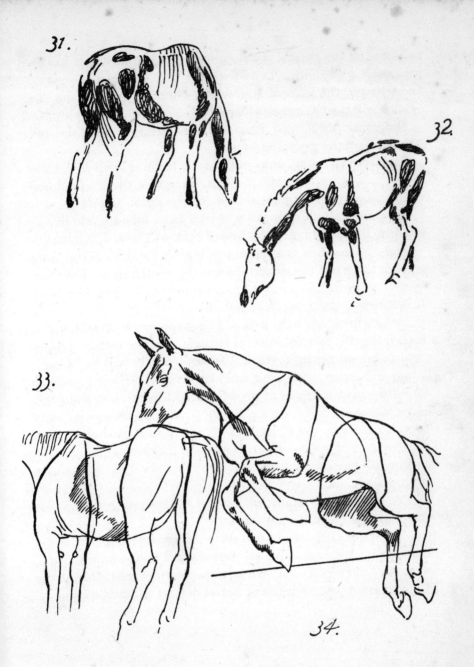

31.

32.

33.

34.

and head in the normal position, seen in Diagrams 1, 2, 3. This position has something to do with the easy dispersal of weight, and whether the horse stands, walks, canters or gallops, the line of back will not change considerably.

Diagrams 35-38 will illustrate this maxim. Note the tail streaming in the galloping horse.

The trotting horse, as a result of his training, will be a little more, as it were, staccato in his striking of attitudes; and one would show the neck more arched and the action arrested.

An animal climbing a hill will lean more forward and downward with the head, and the line of back will be as Diagram 39.

The extension of the spinal column in the neck is just long enough to permit the standing horse (by stretching his head forwards) to graze in comfort. Diagram 40 will show the bony structure as controlling this attitude.

Surface form and colour should be given much consideration, both from the point of view of texture creating colour and the local colour as giving texture. Various textures will be lit variously: and horses, with their hairy covering of different qualities and different directions of growth, might be studied from this angle almost entirely. Again, the local colour markings not only serve to separate the different individuals, but give also a textural quality of great decorative value to the drawing.

The instance of the striping of the zebra is a striking example of this last.

The first consideration will be that of the hair growth as influencing the colour on the form.

A glance at Diagram 41 will show the general tendency of the hair as directed backwards and downwards on the animal with, so to say, three eddies or swirls in the original flow. One at the front of head, between the eyes and down the nose; another at

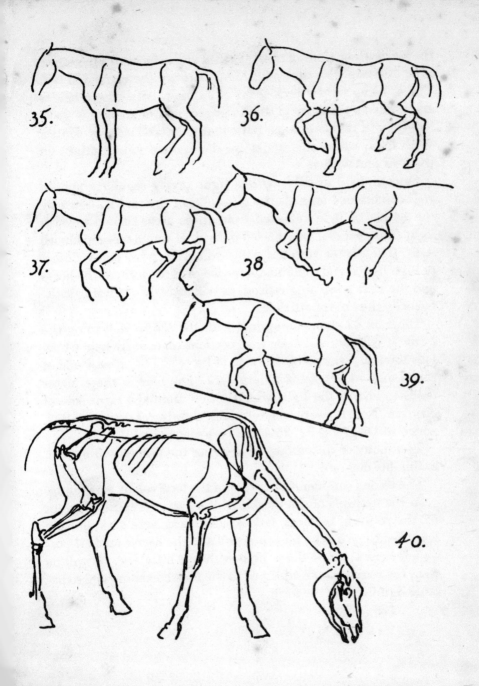

35.

36.

37.

38

39.

40.

the *pectorals* or front of chest; a third at the forward junction of hind quarters with the body. Also, there are the mane and tail. These, being on the back seam of animals, will, where hair is short, have a tendency to stand upright: and, if allowed to grow longer, will divide so as to fall equally on both sides of centre. With foals, where the manes are short, these stand upright on the neck and withers.

Smooth hair usually *reflects* light pretty regularly and in well-conditioned animals the glossiness of the coat is shown by the flashes of light reflected from those areas turned towards light. The coat of a long-haired individual would seem to absorb light. The darker varieties will, ordinarily, have many *flashes* or high lights, and combined knowledge of the form of the horse and the laws governing reflections will assist in rendering satisfactorily the type or attitude.

Diagram 42 shows an animal with the *flashes* indicating the form. It will be recognised that portions covered by hair which falls towards light (as on left side of horse's head, at rear end of barrel and on left *pectoral*) are dark. The hair in these places tends to absorb the light which comes from the right side of diagram. Note the several projections, showing as positive lights, which in Diagrams 22, 23 and 25 are seen as darks.

Testimony of the efficacy of drawing the flashes will be seen in this one diagram.

The second consideration is that of the local colour patterning.

In the example of the markings of a grey, given in Diagram 43, the points of pasterns, fetlocks and hocks were dark, but the light markings on the four quarters and the barrel made it possible for one to draw the animal with but little else. As will be seen, the round spots conformed to the foreshortening and so became significant of the form.

124

41.

42.

Occasionally, enlarged veins will contribute in this way and a few of the most emergent will be seen in Diagram 44.

Another feature should be mentioned; it is the callosity which occurs in members of the horse tribe—sometimes called the chestnut. This shows on each set of limbs differently. On the fore limb it is above the wrist joint, inside the leg; on the hinder, to come just above the fetlock and under the heel, inside the limb.

Chestnuts are shown in Diagrams 1, 2 and 3 of this chapter. With the ass kind the hinder one is, mostly, non-existent and that on the fore limb is higher and smoother than on the horse.

Mention has been made already of the striped zebra. Several other members of the horse tribe have stripes in a lesser degree; the onaga and quagga are more marked than the ass.

There is a legend connecting the markings on the asses' backs with the entry of Christ into Jerusalem. It is said that the cross on the shoulder of this animal is a reminder to posterity of his once having carried crucified Deity, and the mark was in commemoration of this service. Certainly, the Indian wild ass has only a central dark stripe adown the back, and this legend serves to remind one of the distinguishing marks of the ass kind.

ZEBRA One variety of zebra has many crosses, though some are ramified.

Diagram 45 shows a Grant's zebra, defined by means of the distinguishing markings only.

ASS In the British Isles the ass has not been selectively bred to the same perfection as the horse; and, whilst a pretty animal, is small. He is not so heavy about either the quarters or shoulders as the horse—the legs are straighter—in appearance more like the unformed foal of the horse; and, on account of the more upright hoof, he seems to have a mincing gait. The tail is covered with shortish hair, except for a longer tuft at the end, and the

126

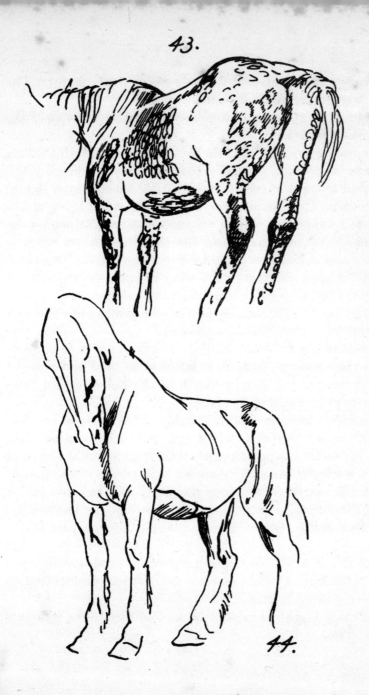

43.

44.

ASS   well-known characteristic of the ears is a special feature. The mane is short and stands upright.

Diagram 46 gives an ass and shows a typical example of the local colour patterning.

HORSES   The rolling eye and ears laid back proclaim a spiteful nature in the horse; though, generally, the ear is used for hearing and is pricked forward, turned outward or laid back to catch significant sounds. This feature may be summarised as being of the shape of a wild arum flower; the tube inserted just behind the attachment of lower jaw, and the sheath extension opening forward and outward at angle seen in Diagram 47. The ear is capable of great rotation in the effort to catch sounds; and the geometric figure seen in this diagram indicates the possible openings at the different sections of the semicircle. The ears move either concurrently or separately.

The side view Diagram 48 shows length of ear to be equivalent to that distance from its attachment to head as far as the inner border of the eye—a fourth of the measurement from upper curve of nostril to tip of ear.

The horse does not express emotion so obviously as the dog. Though to the patient observer and those who tend animals, every mood will be apparent, the casual student will see no more than a noble aloofness and seeming indifference to the human world. On nearly all occasions sensibility will be conveyed by doing something. The features of expression are less mobile; the effect being that of greater placidity on the part of the horse.

The tail, beyond expressing irritation at persistent flies and used in reprimand for the same, is employed for balance and air dispersal when galloping.

Grouping is most satisfactorily done in the studio, though a

128

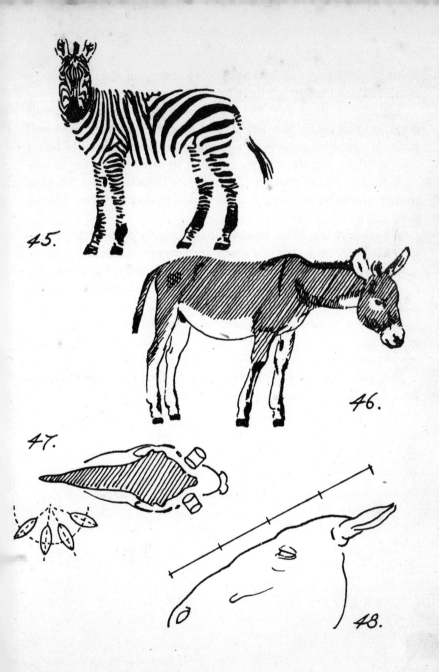

45.

46.

47.

48.

habit of scribbling will make possible notation of the momentary combinations for further development.

The advice given as to the best rendering of an animal on all occasions will be not the less true of groups. The back lines will position and attitudinise the animals—the convex lines of bones should follow and the masses be filled in afterwards. Light and dark animals juxtaposed will always be effective and for that matter the formal tones, *i.e.* those descriptive of form, can be used.

When drawing from animals use a largish piece of paper (or alternatively, make several small drawings on a smaller piece of paper). The animals will return to, approximately, the same attitudes and one can then add any information omitted in the early stages. One can do this with animals more easily than with humans, for their activities are not so varied and, in the event of adding further information from a different individual, types are not so different or so many as with the human kind.

Diagrams 49 and 50 show two notes of the kind suggested and would be augmented should time be available.

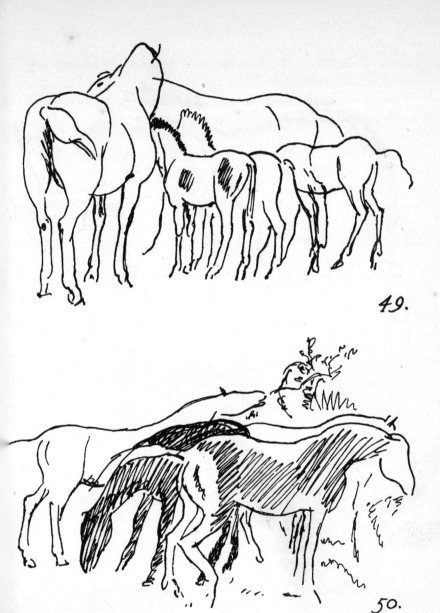

49.

50.

Chapter 6

The Hollow Horns: Oxen, Buffalo, Bison

ANIMAL DRAWING HAS TO BE DONE LARGELY FROM OBSER-
vation or memory. For not only is the student faced with the
restlessness of many kinds of animals during the greater part of
the day, but their size is, at times, an impediment.

Small animals and birds are not so difficult in this way. They
will permit of an easier comprehension of the whole—incident
and relationship are seen with equal facility from the one distance.

Large animals entail separate study of incident and, short of
artificially aided eyesight, the details may not be seen so minutely as with the smaller kinds. This is a mixed blessing; for although it forces one to subordinate the incident to the whole
(and in this any natural circumstances may be regarded as fortunate) there is, ultimately, a tendency for one to get too close
to the animal. One approaches nearer in order to realise the detail but, on a closer investigation, the relationships or proportions are distorted. For example, one might get so close as to see
only the projections and they hide the essential form to which
they attach as buttresses.

A simple way of regulating this distortion is to consider
whether the whole animal may be seen without turning the
head. If it be possible so to view the animal then it might be
taken as granted that the parts will cohere and, at the same
time, provide sufficient detail.

The separate study of smaller detail might be indulged,
though only with a wary eye on its relationship to the whole.

This enquiry into a more detailed information, it must be remembered, is only to enable one to draw with greater confidence.

Attention to the last mentioned truths may prevent a drawing, and not the less an incident, from becoming monstrous.

That the ox kind has been associated with man since the earliest days of human society is borne out by the numerous stories in ancient mythologies. Northern nomads and the Mediterranean peoples all regarded this animal as essential in their agrarian communities.

Quite apart from the utilitarian point of view we have come to regard oxen as part of our countryside and, as sometimes familiarity prevents too close a scrutiny, a brief description is introduced.

Width and 'stockiness' are to be observed in contrast with other animals. Horns are carried by both sexes and oxen have, proportionately, shorter and smaller heads and necks than horses. The divided hoof is formed from the third and fourth toes and the projecting hinder toes (the second and fifth) are very noticeable. Pasterns, sometimes called the feet, are shorter than with the horse.

A generalised cow is shown in Diagram 1 and, though the height of back above shoulders suggests the ox, it will serve as a basis for investigation.

The example chosen resembles closely the familiar beasts of our country. Darker parts in the diagram suggest the undercutting surfaces and these are simplified in the interest of legibility. The udder shows as those peculiar to artificially milked animals of the kind. (That is, supposing the milkmaid to be unnecessary in a wild state.) The upright shoulder, squareness of hind quarters and pendulous flesh under throat and chest are peculiar.

134

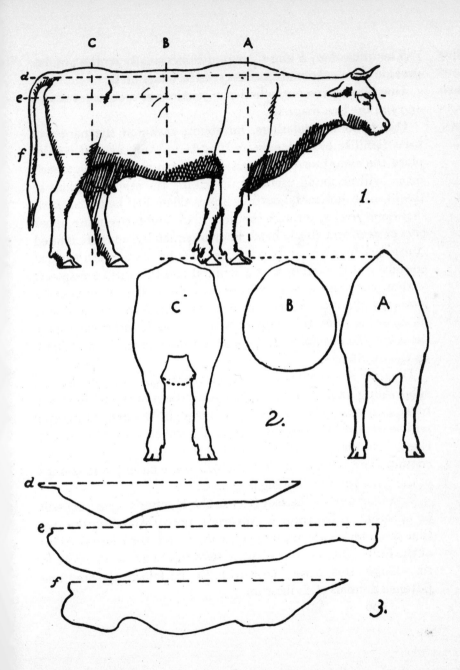

.The lines of *A, B* and *C,* regarded sectionally on the animal, provide the elevational contours seen in Diagram 2.

Diagram 3 gives three half-plan sections as seen at levels *d, e* and *f* in the first diagram.

Our pastoral forefathers, no doubt, invented the names of parts familiar to cattlemen and butchers. And, even if we deplore the slaughter of animals for human food, the butcher's terms will be found useful in describing the several regions of the beast. A horizontal cutting line is taken just below *ischium,* to disjoint *femur,* through shoulder blade and takes in the upper part of neck and all the head. Four unequal divisions are named rump, sirloin, *chine* and neck. The *chine* has its forward vertical boundary at the tallest part of animal and this line corresponds to that part known as the withers in a horse. One other portion is worthy of notice: it is that lower mass of neck in front of shoulder. To it is given the name of 'shaking piece' and it very aptly describes the *dewlap* which depends from the throat and chest on the ox kind.

Diagram 4 was made from a short-horn cow and, whilst the subdividing lines do not pretend the divisions of the professional meat purveyor, the two portions noted in the last paragraph will be seen as between the lines at *X*'s and on neck and front of chest. This diagram was intended as showing a 'basket work' of contours and the various sections will make clear the meanings of the tones in the following diagram.

The shortness of the feet (to use the butcher's term yet) will be apparent in Diagram 5. Apparent, notwithstanding the fact that spectator's view would appear to shorten the other portions of the limb. The peculiar suspension of the barrel is conveyed in this design: this is very noticeable in the selectively-bred and fattened animals of civilisation.

136

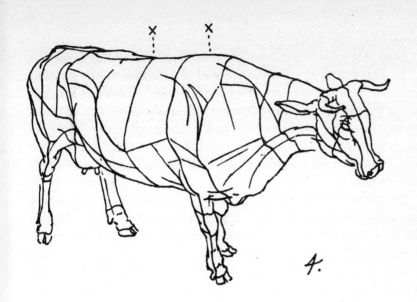

4.

5.

Note, also, the extension of *frontal bone* to carry the horns.

In examining the bony carcase of the ox one might see portions resembling those on the opposite page. These are actually taken from those of a musk ox and, curiously enough, this is not an ox but a link between oxen and goats or antelopes. The goat tail is present and the high flattish hinder ribs; though in other particulars the proportions and details are sufficiently similar to the true ox.

Diagram 6 shows the usual thirteen right ribs of the ox and the wider blade-like forward ribs project in front of shoulder in the way peculiar to the animal. Except for a somewhat greater projection of spinous process in the second *cervical vertebra* and a less upright shoulder blade the likeness is adequate. The eight *sternal* ribs ensure the average proportions of the rib-cage.

Diagram 7 gives axes of ribs seen from the front—the highest one is the twelfth and the longest spinous process of backbones is at about the eighth. *S* in diagram signifies breast bone.

The bony axes of left hinder limb are seen in Diagram 8: these are viewed from the front. The typical ox attitude is here in the outward thrust of knee and the inward turn of heel.

An outside view of the right fore limb is shown in Diagram 9. The shoulder blade has its posterior border at about the seventh rib.

A front view of the same limb is given in Diagram 10. The outward thrust of elbow is not so pronounced in the oxen, but the normal attitudes of standing are conveyed very well by these axes.

Limbs have most movement at their junction with body—at *femoral* and shoulder joints: these are capable of rotation, other joints may be likened to hinges.

The skulls of the ox kind are very different, as can be seen by the examples of buffaloes and bison. Quite apart from functional

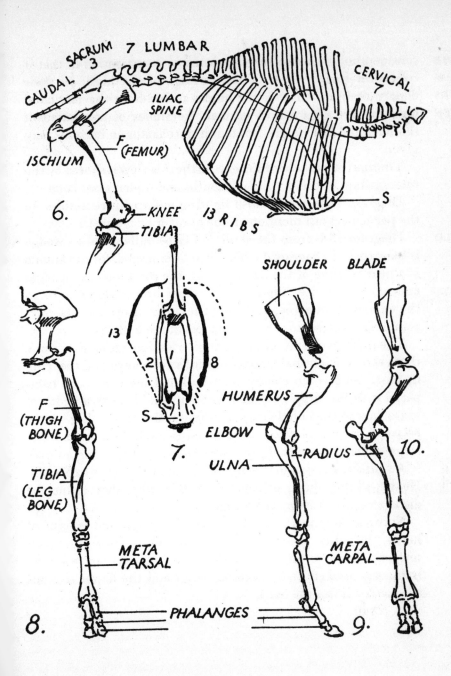

CAUDAL SACRUM 3 7 LUMBAR CERVICAL 7

ILIAC SPINE

ISCHIUM

F (FEMUR)

6.

KNEE

TIBIA

13 RIBS

S

13

2

8

S

7.

F (THIGH BONE)

TIBIA (LEG BONE)

META TARSAL

PHALANGES

8.

SHOULDER BLADE

HUMERUS

ELBOW

ULNA

RADIUS

META CARPAL

PHALANGES

9.

10.

considerations the structure is worthy of investigation in that it influences surface form, if not carriage of the head. In their departure from vertical, the angles of heads in the left hand diagrams are regarded as normal. Reminder of association of shoulder and head angles posited in the chapter on horses is here given.

The most remarkable difference in the side view is shown by the relationships of the cavities of mouths and under *nasal* bones.

Diagram 11 is of a Spanish fighting bull and it resembles, in the particulars last mentioned, the bison of Diagram 15.

Diagram 13 is from the skull of a Cape buffalo and its wedge is liker that of Diagram 11 (this is to be expected, for the buffalo is a near relative of the ox) although the combinations of nasal

and mouth cavities differ. The 'rocking' lines of lower jaws in the ox and bison agree, as do also the *orbits* or eye sockets. Surrounding processes to orbit project less in the buffalo.

The three diagrams on the right give 'end on' views of the same three skulls. Right halves only of skulls are shown and the 'rise' in nasal bones with the Spanish bull and bison is to be compared with the 'drop' in that of the buffalo. The extra width of lower jaw in the buffalo only emphasises the contrasting widths between horns and *orbits* seen in the two other diagrams. The ridge of cheek bone is of great significance in the living animal.

Attention is drawn to the differences in horns of the ox family. Heavy, slight, blunt, polished or buckler-like, they cannot be disregarded in drawing the animal.

Notwithstanding the great variety in design and weight of horns, the actual growth of horns is constant. They grow both towards the ends and sectionally. That is, circular sectioned horns are marked by corrugating rings and the flatter sections are *banded across* the horn.

140

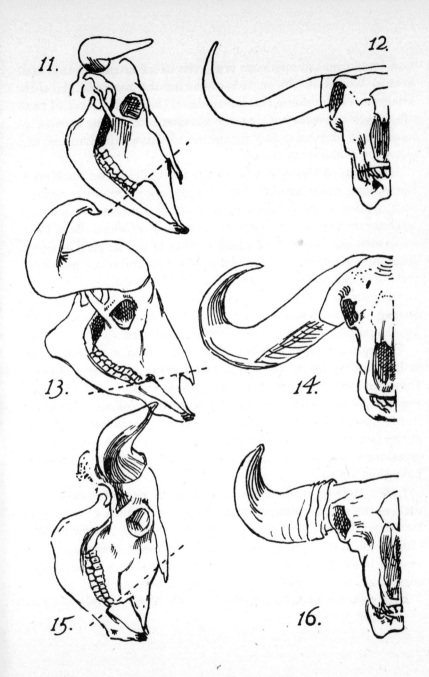

11.

12.

13.

14.

15.

16.

A few formal comparisons are given in the accompanying diagrams. Except in the matter of horns, the example given in Diagram 17 resembles the type of head shown at the top of previous page. *Frontal* bone and eye-socket projections, as well as *nasal* bone and lower jaw formation of this young banting ox, show the character of the ox.

Diagram 18 shows a side view of a buffalo; the bucklered horns, long *nasal* bone and peculiar jaw are structurally significant, while the dropping ear is an essential characteristic.

Diagram 19 is a front view of the head of a Cape buffalo, held in an attitude similar to the half-skull of Diagram 14. The bony formation already noted is seen to exert its influence here and the horns and ears should be remembered as peculiar.

Diagram 20 gives an 'end on' view of a bison's head. The projecting eye, formation of horn, 'rise' of *nasal* bone, width of cheek and narrowness of lower jaw are indicated.

Diagram 21 shows another view of the head of a bison. This is held rather lower and the kind of horn and projections of cheek and eye socket are clearly expressed. Hair grows low on the nose of the bison, though the oxen and buffaloes have bare noses. Bison differ in other details from the remaining members of the family and the most remarkable is that of the longer body occasioned by fourteen or fifteen pairs of ribs (other members have thirteen pairs).

Action may be studied from the point of view of association, such as the animal manoeuvring differently amidst a variety of landscape details. This might result in unusual or queer attitudes. Again, the familiar action of the ordinary, everyday business of feeding, ruminating, drinking or walking could, with advantage, prove the basis of one's investigations.

Both of these approaches will be made easier by following a

142

17.

18.

19.

20.

21.

rational enquiry and adopting the habit of observing *repeatedly* the same formal combinations.

The normal action of an ox in walking—the head is 'bobbed' in time to the alternate moves of the fore-legs—the 'throwing' of the head backwards at some irritation on the shoulder, the bending of the fore-legs first in settling down to ruminate and again commencing to rise at the hinder end, these are all worthy of the draughtsman's expression.

Form will conduce towards some attitudes as, for instance, with the flattish surface under body and the almost unvarying line from knee to foot. These combine inevitably to give the usual ruminating attitude.

Diagrams 22 to 25 give a slight idea of the significance of the last mentioned structural influence on the attitude whilst ruminating. The tilts of *pelves* and uprightness of barrels are dictated by anatomical facts.

Diagrams 26 and 27 give the grazing and chastising of flies attitudes. The latter illustrates the 'short reach' of the neck and head.

These are both from animals of a hot country and show the characteristics of animals not bred in rich pasture land. They resemble more the ranging animals of extensive and dry plains. The slimness of hind quarters is one noticeable mark of the influence of feeding on the animal.

In this respect, Diagrams 26 and 27 may be likened to wild animals.

Texture is the term given to all variations of surface—the weaving, knitting or interplay of hair as also the polish of a horn, the dustiness or bloom of a hoof or the wetness of nostrils. Again, the coruscations consequent to these surfaces being smooth or rough, wavy or straight, are regarded as texture.

Now, independent of technical means or manner, appreciation

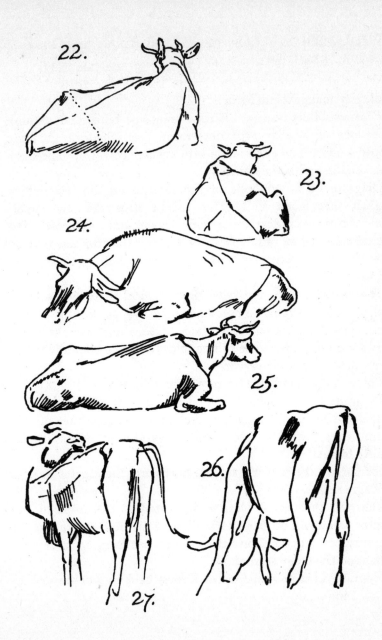

of textures will give style and expression to the draughtsman. Facility in study will be enjoyed by one who analyses truly.

We might subdivide texture into three main parts—superficial, physiological and formal.

Texture differs on the different breeds or kinds and, though conditions of locality will determine this, the draughtsman should study texture to enable him greater power of expression when dealing with the animal.

Diagram 28 is symbolic of the texture on the head of an English short-horn bull. This might illustrate the superficial texture—as describing hair, horn and wet nose. The animal is looked at rather from below and the 'fur' on *frontal*, nose and cheek contrasts with the shorter hair on nose, jaws and neck.

That which might be styled physiological texture is seen in Diagram 29: the veins on nose and above eye, as also the 'colour' of the eye, determine the surface texture and are the cause more than the texture itself. The folds in the dewlap might also be grouped with these textures.

This example is from a Mysore humped cow.

Diagram 30 shows some formal textures. It gives a development from an earlier diagram and the radiating lines of skin around eyes, 'shells' of ears and rings around horns are definitely formal.

Formal are the textures on the horns and the creases in neck of Diagram 29.

BISON   The hair texture of bison is indicated at the front of this chapter and again on page 143. That of the bull and calf at the beginning of chapter shows the winter coat hanging in clogged ribbons on the older animal.

BUFFALO   Mention must be made of the almost bald wild or water buf-

146

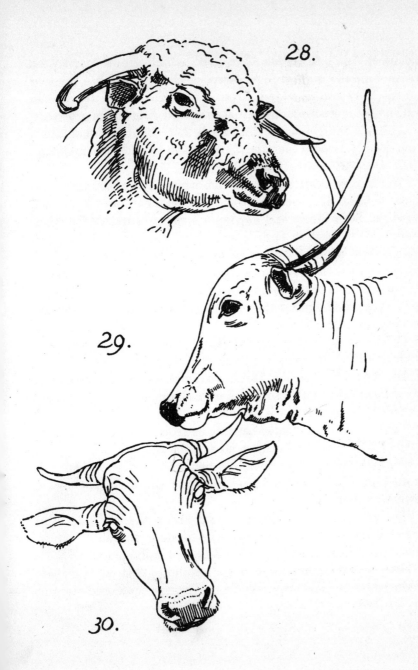

28.

29.

30.

faloes of Asia and Africa. The hair, which grows sparsely on these animals, is differently directed: that of Asia has the hair on the body and shoulders directed forwards, while the African variety is covered with the usual rearward direction of growth.

Animals indigenous to uniformly hot countries maintain a consistently smooth coat and those native to colder parts change their coats with the seasons.

The humped cattle of India and other oriental countries and those animals of Africa and the Mediterranean have developed dewlaps. Both hump and dewlap are nature's device for withstanding the possible famine or meagre feeding periods. With many kinds of animals, native to countries liable to seasons of want, some such provision is made. (The example of the camel is, perhaps, one of the best known, and many species of antelopes are so protected against the lean days.) These humped animals are usually pale in colour.

Colour, considered as contributing decoratively to form, is of interest to the draughtsman, and the Hirsar humped bull from India, shown in Diagram 31, is an example of delicate colouring. He is light fawn with a soft darker gradation on the back, hump and neck; horns and hoofs are black.

The young domesticated banting ox from Malay, seen in Diagram 32, is brown with darker nose, hoofs and tail tuft.

Diagram 33 gives another humped animal, the Gujerat bull from India. He is white under and light and dark grey above, with black horns.

The wild banting in Malay and Java show the white circle on the rump which occurs on many wild herding ruminants, whilst this is not perpetuated in the domesticated individuals.

History and legend point to the possibility that white or pale coloured cattle came originally from Egypt or equatorial regions.

148

31.

32.

33.

Obviously, it is impossible for us to know the prevailing colour of the prehistoric ox; and those colour renderings done by prehistoric man in caves were, in all probability, of a significance other than imitative. (What coloured records do exist seem to have been done during a later ice age and the bison figures largely in these.) Bison and northern oxen, it may be inferred, were always dark.

Many of the breeds known in domestication are blotched or mottled and their markings are of interest to the draughtsman.

Regarding the colour or colours as values, they are serviceable in the degree to which they signalise form or attitude; and it is a remarkable fact that most animals may be symbolised by these values alone.

The short-horn varieties seen in Diagrams 34 to 38 are examples of values denoting form.

Diagram 37, though fragmentary and slight, conveys a maximum expressiveness and the still slighter fragment of Diagram 38 is significant of the reclining hinder quarters of a cow.

The grouping of animals may be made attractive by an arrangement of values, for to both form and composition might be given that variety which evokes interest if not enthusiasm.

The term values must not be mistaken for those accidents of light and shade which, as they are the result of momentary conditions, have been ignored in these notes.

Some modelling, naturally, will be found of assistance, but only in the emphasis given to form and chosen with intent to avoid distraction in expressiveness.

150

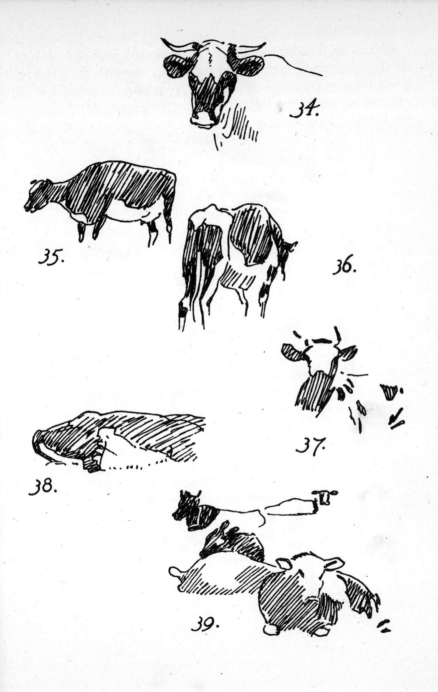

34.

35.

36.

37.

38.

39.

Chapter 7

The Hollow Horns: Goats, Sheep

GOATS AND SHEEP ARE, NATIVELY, INHABITANTS OF THE mountain slopes and rocks.

Wild sheep resemble the goat more closely than those breeds of civilised man, and the cultivated sheep as he is known in Europe, Australia and America is quite different from those of Asia and Africa. These last seem more akin to the goat in form and colour and, as a point of comparison, one might consider that eastern peoples keep the more primitive herds—they are not *wool* producers.

Sheep and goats are toe walkers and, as with all *digitigrades*, the hoofs are more upright when the animal inhabits a hard or rocky landscape.

Many of the sheep have a long hair-like covering, though this is only a development consequent to their constant exposure to rain or snow. Examination under the microscope would reveal the barbs which occur on all wool threads and so mark the sheep as distinct from the goat. Those closely related animals of South America—the guanacos, llamas, vicunas and alpacas have similar coats to the sheep.

Sheep feed on grass while the goat feeds on leaves and twigs. Both kinds grow horns, though in many breeds of sheep only the males carry them. Broadly speaking, the horns of goats are curved or spiral in one plane only, whilst the sheep kind have coiled or shell-formed horns: though it is true that some species of sheep have horns closely resembling those of the goat kind.

Very broadly, the goats may be likened to the antelope kind

whilst the sheep more nearly resemble deer. These divisions will be clear on investigating both the forms of body and horns.

The goat-sheep kind is to be divided into many varieties. From the mouflon (which is probably the progenitor of all cultivated breeds of sheep) through the Barbary sheep to the true goat: and, on the other side, to all the kinds of sheep bred by man.

The example shown in Diagram 1 of this chapter is that of the ibex; and it displays characteristics of both the goat and sheep kinds.

The skull is bluntly wedge-shaped, eyes are high and under the horns, a chin beard is carried and the neck is long. Horns are in one plane and the after ribs are wide. Hoofs are *high* and, in proximity, its odour establishes its claim to be a goat. Over all, the coat is a hairy one.

Elevational sections of this animal are seen in Diagram 2, and the extra widths of barrel and hind quarters will be noticed.

Diagram 3 gives the proportions of the true sheep, though not of any one particular breed. Differences are to be seen in neck, which is shorter than with the goat; the eye is lower, legs are stouter and short, upper lip does not project so far in front of nostril, shoulder is more upright and the barrel is heavier towards shoulder.

The significance of the line of back will be appreciated and it must be urged again that the habit of drawing this line first is a good one. Even if mathematical accuracy is not attained when drawing from the living animal this custom will make the student observe carefully. The *forward* and bony lines of limbs should be added in order both to characterise the kind and memorise the gait. The modelling of the undersides helps in noting projections and mass.

154

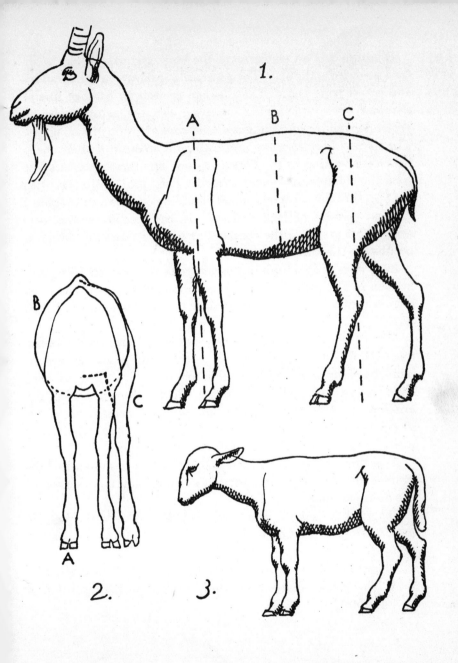

1.

A B C

B

C

A

2.

3.

Diagram 4 is an elevation of the bony framework of a male ibex, seen from the side. The goat build is shown in the shoulder and breast bone angle. The rib-cage projects in front of line of shoulder blade and head of *humerus*: also, the *pelvis* is seen to protrude well beyond the *sacral* and *caudal* group of backbones. The spines of *vertebræ* are interesting on account of their sharp backward leaning in the *dorsal* region. The most upright spine is on the thirteenth *dorsal vertebra*. (This would argue, as with the dog, that the point of greatest rounding occurs in this region.) A great spinous projection is seen in the second *cervical vertebra*. This gives, to the contours of neck, a character which is peculiar to the kind.

Bony axes of fore limb in the natural attitude of standing will be seen in Diagram 5. This is seen from the front and the twist outwards of both *scapula* (or shoulder blade) and *humerus* will be noted.

A front view of the left hinder is seen in Diagram 6 and the outward thrust of knee, as well as the wide *pelvis*, is typical. This widening of the *pelvic* region, together with the downward tilt of breast bone, gives a character which is reminiscent of the antelope kind. In the sheep the *sternum*, or breast bone, is not so noticeably dropped to the rear. Hence the grouping with the deer—mentioned at the beginning of this chapter.

A section of barrel at about the eighth rib is shown in Diagram 7 and the straighter portion of same may be observed in the living animal.

Diagram 8 shows a rear view of *pelvis*. The 'drop' will be noticed and the relation to the spinous process of the last *lumbar vertebra*.

Diagram 9 shows a side elevation of the skull of a Siberian ibex. The wedge shape is peculiar, as also the high position of

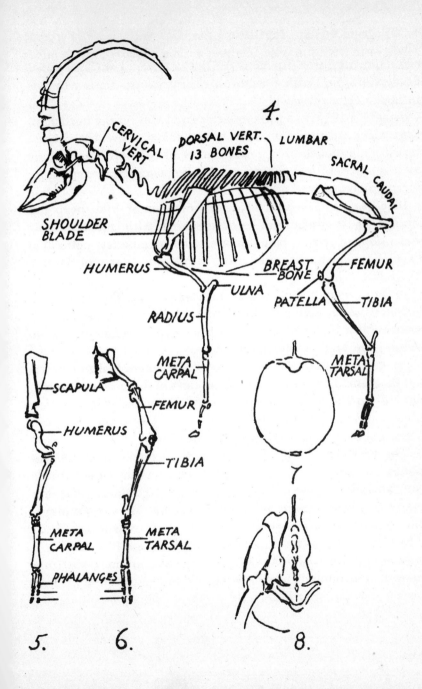

4.

CERVICAL VERT

DORSAL VERT. 13 BONES

LUMBAR

SACRAL CAUDAL

SHOULDER BLADE

HUMERUS

BREAST BONE

FEMUR

ULNA

PATELLA

TIBIA

RADIUS

META CARPAL

META TARSAL

SCAPULA

FEMUR

HUMERUS

TIBIA

META CARPAL

META TARSAL

PHALANGES

5.

6.

7.

8.

orbit and the three directions in line of lower jaw. The upper borders of *orbit*, with *frontal bone*, buttress the horn which is immediately above *orbit*.

Diagram 10 gives a three-quarter front view of the head of an ibex which, though seen from rather below, shows the characteristics mentioned. The lower border of *orbit* with *zygomatic* arch is apparent and the widened upper *maxillary*, containing teeth, influences surface also.

The head, in Diagram 11, is of a mouflon or wild sheep and similar characteristics are to be observed. Although the backward slope of *frontal* bone to base of horn and a less noticeable 'wedge' is shown, the other points correspond closely in the two diagrams.

A front view of skull is seen in Diagram 12. This shows the peculiar *orbital* angle and the central ridge to *frontal* bone. A sectional line has been taken over the *maxillaries* and *nasal bone* to show the 'rise' of *nasal bone*.

Diagram 13 shows the influence of the salient features in the last diagram. The eyes are set at the sides of the head and in this differ from the predatory animals. All the grazing animals are capable of seeing largely to the rear as well as to the front and sides, and the setting of the eye permits this.

The drawing of animals involves the exercise of much patience during one's study. Though it be true that some animals can be studied here in enclosed zoological gardens, there are many which may be found amidst more natural surroundings. The draughtsman in search of animals to draw will have least difficulty in finding those cultivated or domesticated kinds.

Whilst it can hardly be said that domestic animals exist in a natural environment, it will be clear that one unsuited to their health and comfort will be unfit for them. This is fortunate, for

9.

10.

11.

12.

13.

the student will, in pursuit of information, become aware of the most suitable locality in which the animals may be found and will not, thenceforth, introduce them into unnatural landscape settings.

In determining those things contributing to give the special character of the animal, one should note the peculiar form and carriage of the horns. The usual section is triangular, and this triangle is set with one side towards the front. The opposite angle is more or less to the side or back according to the species.

Some horns are rounder in section. Horns vary in section, curve and direction and, though it be generally true that the goat kind has horns curving in one direction and that sheep carry horns which spiral *away* to the sides of the head, there are exceptions.

GOATS   Diagram 14 shows the horns of an Angora goat. The longest side of the triangular section is to the front and outwards.

Diagram 15 gives the triangular section of ibex horns and the acute angle is towards front.

The horns given in the two figures of Diagram 16 have blade-like ends. When facing the head, one might hold the left horn in the right hand and turn as though loosening an ordinary screw, moving the thumb inwards and downwards. The two figures show male and female of a common goat and the females have slighter and more ribbed horns. These and Diagram 14 show similar twist.

Diagram 17 shows the chamois horns leaning forwards, though hooked backwards and outwards.

SHEEP   Diagrams 18, 19 and 20 show merino sheep, Derby sheep and mouflon, respectively.

GOATS   Though goat-like in habits, the chamois is not a true goat but an antelope.

160

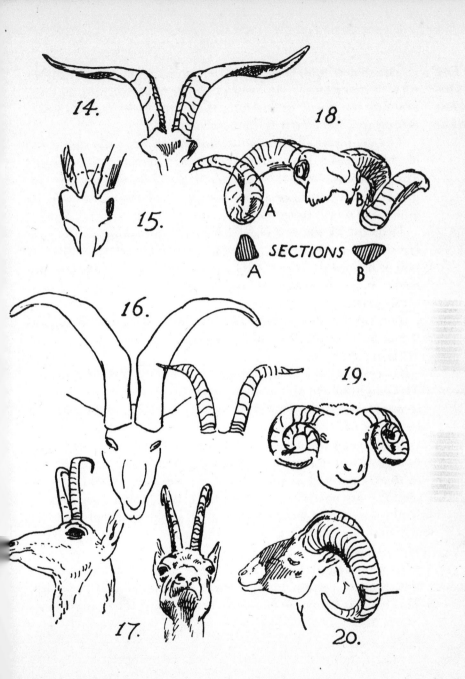

14.

15.

18.

A

SECTIONS

A   B

B

16.

19.

17.

20.

The shell or spiral is proper to sheep horns and the coil will be easy to memorise if one imagines oneself facing the animal, grasping the horns and turning the arms outwards, backwards, downwards and forwards, continuously.

The young of all ruminants, unformed, ungainly and timid as they appear, have strongly-marked characteristics. Formal things are as clear as the local colour markings and the few diagrams on the opposite page show some of the differences by which one might recognise the forms.

GOATS   Diagram 21 shows a kid Barbary sheep basking in the sun. He rests on a rock which, as he is a *goat*, is a proper setting. It will be noticed that the eye is high and the head is of the peculiar wedge shape of goats. The neck is long and the shoulder is not very upright.

The kid thar of Diagram 22 is similarly environed. Below his throat may be seen the influence of ribs and breast bone: shoulder is behind these.

Diagram 23 is a kid of the goat commonly kept in England. The height of eye and divided upper lip mark his kind, even if it were not for the length of neck and formal peculiarities of backbone and shoulder.

SHEEP   Diagram 24 is from the lamb of a mouflon sheep. The woolly coat gives to the form a rounder appearance and, although not so thickly covered as the cultivated kinds, the animal does resemble more nearly the lambs of the better known varieties.

A young llama is seen in Diagram 25 and, except that legs and neck are longer, the head and coat contribute to make it very sheep-like.

As protested earlier in this treatise, action and attitude are the result of certain mathematical combinations of structure. This truth is known to anatomists and, whilst the draughtsman

21.

22.

23.

24.

25.

need not be too enquiring a physiologist, a familiarity with the habits of animals is essential to a personal rendering. The successful draughtsman will have a highly developed critical sense. The animal draughtsman must be acquainted with the animal as he can only otherwise repeat the unenterprising side view or give a dull transcript of the already casual photograph.

The carriage of a head, drooping of the ears, the lifting of a leg, the play or snug ling of the young animals, the reclining attitudes are all intimate and particular. Only the keen observer of the living animal may describe these things with confidence and this confidence is the reward of diligent and watchful patience.

GOATS

Diagram 26 shows a female Barbary sheep with kid. They are seen rather from below and the lucky moment provided a decorative arrangement. The dam expresses solicitude in her attitude and the youngster takes what comfort he is permitted.

The kid thar in Diagram 27 stage a mimic battle and assume the attitudes of the adults under more serious conditions.

SHEEP

Diagram 28 gives the typical sheep attitude; with legs, back, neck and ears suggestive of indecision if not lassitude.

The familiar and usual possesses less interest for the casual observer than for the enquiring; and it must be divulged that very often the apparently uninspiring object provides material for an exciting drawing.

The simple attitude seen in Diagram 29 proved full of information to the draughtsman. It is from a Spanish sheep and the bent fore-leg occasioned the shoulder to drop on that side.

Animal forms are made to appear more subtle by the hair which covers them and, although this sometimes seems to hide the form, ease of movement and ventilation of skin require that the coat design shall be suitable. Animals are closely covered

164

over those large outside tracts and the *lay* of the hair directs the offcasting of rain, snow or dew. There are channels between the hair tracts which permit greatest ease in movement and the necessary passage of air in cooling the animal. The student who is conscious of these facts will, besides giving veracity to his drawings, be much entertained in apportioning their services to the different hair groups.

GOATS

Diagram 30 shows hair grouping and *lay* on the surfaces of two gambolling kids. This is diagrammatic and would be much finer and closer on the living animals. The 'star' on front of head; neck and shoulder groups; front of shoulder, elbow and *radial* groups; *dorsal*, flank, knee, buttock and heel groups are expressive of, rather than disguising form.

Diagram 31 gives a side view of goat's head, the horns of which are from the same animal as Diagram 16. The wedge form of head is seen clearly through the heavy hair growth on jaw and chin.

Attention is called to the usual *pale eye* of the goat-sheep kind —the horizontal pupil is typical. Those nearly antelope kinds, such as the chamoix, have dark eyes.

SHEEP

Diagram 32, of grazing sheep, shows the 'break' in hair. This is more apparent with the wool-covered animals and marks the *living* animal and its actions. The 'break' is full of interest to the designer and supplies him with great textural 'values'.

Colour, or the distinctive *patterning* of animals, assists in typifying the kinds as well as in amplifying the formal statement and it is true that certain forms are more readily recognised by their 'colour'.

The cultivated kinds of sheep in their different colouring undoubtedly show traces of their descent from the wild kinds. One common variety is that of the black-faced and black-legged

30.

31.

32.

sheep. Diagram 33 is descriptive of this and the 'breaks' will be seen as of formal significance.

Several goats are given in Diagram 34 and the great diversity of markings in these animals might suggest nature's attempt to suit the animal's colouring to a constantly changing landscape. The result has been less disastrous than in the sad case of the chameleon when placed upon a piece of tartan.

Diagram 35 gives the 'colour' of the mouflon and although recent varieties show a white patch on the back this is an abnormality or may be an effort at winter covering.

Albinos are individuals with insufficient pigmentation and, as such, are abnormal, though the seasonal change takes place constantly with many kinds and species living in arctic or near arctic zones.

The lower borders of the light upper part of the mouflon are dark and seem to separate the white undersides from the coloured upper surfaces. There are dark patches on inner sides of heel and front of fore-legs. The white circle on rump is carried by many of the herding ruminants. This distinctive marking of the ruminant wild kinds does not seem to be perpetuated in domesticated breeds.

When drawing the gregarious animals it will be interesting, if not essential, to study their social habits. Grouping of the individuals will be constant and this grouping may be caused by several well-marked impulses.

A systematic investigation into motives might, with advantage, govern one's study of animal groups.

A herded group will usually be distinguished by the parallel or radiating formation of the individuals; one such is seen in Diagram 36. This shows some sheep indigenous to a hot country, as will be seen by the slightness of the build and the drooping ears.

33.

34.

35.

Diagram 37 gives a feeding group and shows the familiar V-shaped arrangement of the animals. They are the sheep of rich feeding grounds in a northern country—heavy, placid and well protected by wool.

Diagram 38 shows the mutual-protection group. The rubbing coats seem to afford them the assurance that others of their kind are near, whilst the senses of hearing, seeing and smelling are exercised to the full in the effort to gauge the intentions of the enemy.

This is a more or less radiating arrangement—according to the size of the group.

Resting in the shade is expressed by the grouping of the Spanish goats in Diagram 39. The group is triangular in shape and it is a curious fact that this common impulse always does give the triangle.

Inertia is written all over the three groups seen in Diagrams 39, 40 and 41. They all show the triangle and Diagram 40 has been subdivided into two triangles. The animals are kept for milking purposes and the peculiar attitude is adopted for comfort.

Diagram 41 is more informative than the two previous ones in this respect.

Sparse provender and heat have together prevented the animals from acquiring either adipose flesh or abundant hairy covering.

36.

38.

37.

39.

40.   41.

Chapter 8

The Hollow Horns: Antelopes

ANTELOPES ARE AMONGST THE MOST BEAUTIFUL OF CREA-
tures and, except for very few members of the family, inhabit
the African continent. They are wild animals and, in the scheme
of nature, frequent those regions of rapid vegetable growth.
This is kept within prescribed limits by the fleet and far-ranging
animals of the antelope family.

Antelopes are herding animals and change their feeding
grounds with the seasons.

Nature has ordained that, in their migrations, the animals
should travel by night. This arrangement permits them to
travel the long distances necessary without the enticement of
feeding by the way: and again, the fatigue of the journey is not
so great as would be consequent on travelling during the heat of
the tropical day.

As might be expected of animals living amidst such varied
surroundings as are to be met with in Africa, antelopes differ
considerably in form and colour. In some, the hair coat resembles that of eastern cattle; some are deer-like in texture;
colours vary from pale fawn to rich red and black, and the peculiar markings are no less diverse than the shapes of horns or
varieties of structure proper to the antelope kind. Yet, different
though they be, there are features held in common which separate them from all other kinds.

Usually, both sexes carry horns, though females of the water
buck are without them. The horns are longer and more slender
than with other animals and though some may seem rather

ox-like, their horns are never so simply curved or smooth as those of the oxen. The horns carried by the females of gazelles are slimmer and straighter than those of the males.

Antelopes comprise all the hollow-horned ruminants excepting oxen, sheep and goats; and, as there are some hundreds of species, one would expect so universal a term as antelope to cover many seemingly different families.

The typical antelope or gazelle form is given in Diagram 1 and it does not represent any one species.

For greater ease in describing, this diagram is contrasted with those others introducing the deer and goat-sheep forms in chapters 4 and 7.

Comparisons deal with proportions and refer to the *average* types.

Hind quarters, or croup, is high with antelopes; the *dorsal* region is high with the goat and the shoulders with the deer. The neck is longer than with the goat kind and the tail is longer than with either goat or deer, though not so long as with oxen. Shoulders are not so upright as with deer, but approximate the angle of goats'. The front, or throat border of shoulder, is sometimes in front of rib-cage at neck, whilst the horns have closer resemblance to goats than to other ruminants.

With many species, the walking toes project forwards more than in goats; *pasterns* are long and the *dew toes* are more noticeable than with the goat-sheep kind.

The sections in Diagram 2 show differences (marked) in contrast with the other hollow horns.

Section *A* shows as flatter at top between shoulders. Fore-legs are slim and more directed inwards, towards wrist, than in deer.

The relationship in heights of sections *B* and *C* differ from those seen in the deer and goat chapters. The croup (*C*) is

174

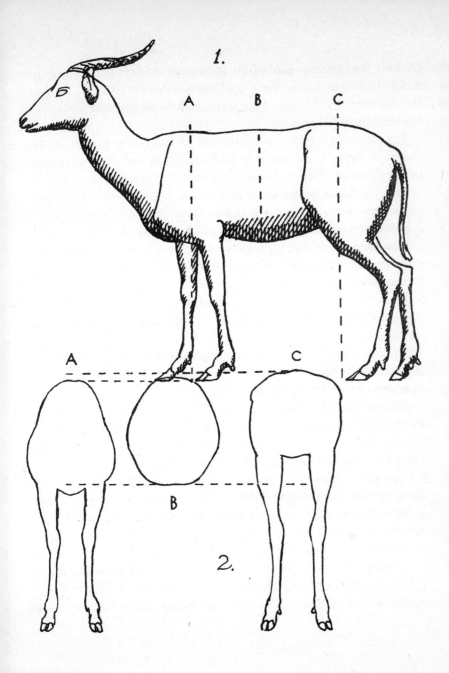

1.

A   B   C

A   C

B

2.

highest, and a remarkable difference is seen in the formation of the whole hind quarters. The top of croup is wider (that is, further from centre) than knee: the goat, it will be remembered, has the knee thrust outwards.

Diagram 3 gives the peculiarities of bony axes proper to the antelope type; shoulder is well forward, breast well back and *pelvis* dropped. The 'rocking' line of lower jaw is not so noticeable as with the goats and is reminiscent of the deer. The composite line of *dorsal* spines is not so variable as with the deer and is graduated onto neck by the spines of *cervical vertebræ*.

The *deep* pelvis and high knee contribute towards the rounder quarters of antelope, whilst the whole curving length of hinder limb gives that resilience and strength which is known to be invested in arch forms. In contrast to this one might refer to the similar local peculiarities of the goat as giving great springing powers.

Diagram 4 shows the strong, spirally twisted horns of the eland and the spiral rings have an outward twist from the skull upwards (when facing the animal).

Animals such as the gazelles, bush buck, gemsbok or oryx and the lesser kudu have slender, long and strongly ringed horns: whilst the bontebok or hartebeest, kudu, bongo, sable and harnessed antelopes have twisted and stouter horns.

The very curious Neumann's hartebeest carries short, curved horns which are strongly ribbed to about half their length. Their form is given in Diagrams 5 and 6. As will be seen, the skull is very narrow when viewed from the front, and Diagram 6 shows the twist and ridges of horn as seen from the side.

Another narrow headed, horn carrying antelope is known as the Hunter's antelope. This is diagrammatised at figures 7 and 8, the upper portions only of skulls being given. The symbols

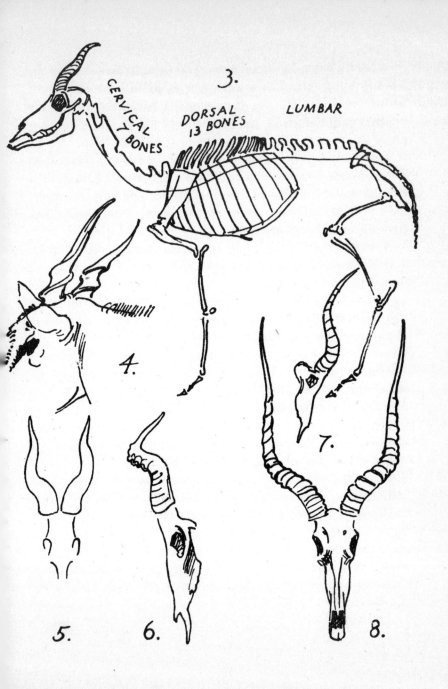

3.

CERVICAL
7 BONES

DORSAL
13 BONES

LUMBAR

4.

5.   6.   7.   8.

used for the horns are seen to suggest the *movement* of the twist and, quite apart from the colour or modelling which would be added, determine the design of growth.

Some variations from the normal type are seen on the opposite page.

That of Diagram 9 is a nylghai and its curious form is occasioned by the height at shoulders and shortness of neck. It carries the round buttocks of the antelope and the forward reaching toes; but the long tail, tall shoulders, spotted ears and forward curving small horns are peculiar.

A strange combination will be seen in Diagram 10—it is from a wildebeest or gnu. The high, flat and downward curving horns; the smooth, broad muzzle and the heaviness of shoulder and neck suggest close relationship with the ox, as do also the sturdiness of the hoofs and *pasterns*. He is decorated with fans of hair on the nose, chin, throat and chest and his mane and tail recalls the horse.

The enumerated characteristics resemble the heraldic symbol of the unicorn, and to a timid or distant discoverer might well have looked like the small silhouette. That the figure known as a co-supporter to the lion in the British Royal Arms does suggest this, might be taken as an indication of the questionable veracity of the early travellers' tales. And, far from blaming the supposed pioneers, the author can vouch for the intimidating effect of the 'gambols' of certain wildebeest sentries.

Diagram 11 shows the Neumann's hartebeest alluded to earlier. His quarters are slimmer than with the normal antelope and the height of shoulder, as well as its 'upright' angle, gives him an odd appearance. The height of *frontal* bone, narrow and tapering muzzle and great elevation of the short curved horns are peculiar.

178

9.

10.

11.

It will be a pity if all these strange creatures disappear for the want of controlled reserves, and it ought to be deplored that either the animals survive unhappily in confinement, or are travestied in stuffed specimens.

Action, it must be remembered, is mathematical and determined by the underlying bony structure more than by the will of the animal. The resting position peculiar to the antelope differs from that of the ox kind by *reason of* the bony axes. The rearward 'drop' of *pelvis* and rounder quarters combine to rest differently on the ground when the antelope is at rest. Also, in this position, the shoulder-and-back line differs from that of deer. There is a more gradual drop towards neck insertion which shows the body as a more compacted and rounder mass than that of the deer.

The kudu of Diagram 12 shows very clearly the rounding of the quarters when resting. He is a striped animal with a mane, long throat tuft and spiral horns.

The young gazelle in Diagram 13 illustrates the peculiarities of the antelope type, and he has face glands and upright hoofs. These last because of his dry locality.

Diagram 14 gives a lechwe antelope from N.W. Africa. The attitude demonstrates the structural influence of the croup and hinder limb. This animal is fulvous on the back with darker marks down the front of fore-legs and again to the outer sides of the hinders. Face glands are present, as with many of the antelopes, and he is white around eye, underneath body and inside the legs.

The carriage of head and neck is not such a high one as with the deer. In the first place, the horns are not so heavy as antlers nor is the angle of growth so upright.

Their action in walking approaches the trot with, as it were, a diagonal pull; *e.g.* right fore-leg and left hinder, and left fore-

180

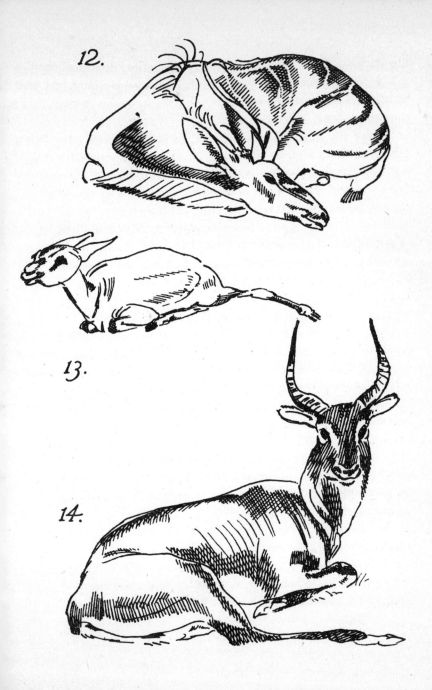

12.

13.

14.

leg working with the right hinder. Probably, this combination makes for staying power in their protracted migrations.

Hair texture may be used advantageously when drawing certain antelopes.

One of the most interesting designs is that of the gnu, and a young male is seen in Diagram 15. Young, because his horns are straighter and slimmer than they would be if he were an older animal. He is of the brindled variety; and the example shown in Diagram 10 was of a white-tailed gnu.

There are several varieties of texture on this animal: the short smooth hair of the general coat; the longer silky smoothness around the front of feet; the matt of *frontal* and *nasal* areas on head; the bristly festoons of mane and tail and the chin and throat tuft.

As may be seen, he makes an attractive linear design.

The powerful eland, shown in Diagram 16, is the largest of the antelopes and he is handsomely striped. His hair texture might be considered as independent of the colour and the matt between eyes gives a special character to the head.

The eland's nose is bare and he carries a dewlap upon which, in front of the throat, is to be seen a tuft of hair. His black mane and the bushy end to tail are peculiar features, whilst allusion to the spirally-ringed horns has been made already.

Diagram 17 gives a female water buck (hornless) and the toes are much elongated and widened to permit its walking on floating herbage.

The white circles on the rumps of these water buck, though usually present, are sometimes only in outline.

A ruff is worn and the forward tendency of hair on shoulders is peculiar, as also the central 'peak' at the meeting of the two directions on sides of neck and front of chest.

182

THE
HOLLOW
HORNS
ANTELOPES

The diagram should not be considered as representational, but the hair read as directional.

Textures of two kinds are seen in Diagrams 18 and 19, and Diagram 20 combines both of these. The animal is a white-eared kob from the Upper Nile.

Diagram 18 shows the features of local colour: white ears, cheek and throat spots, chest, belly and inside limbs and tail; dark upper parts and outside markings on limbs and feet; as well as black horns and toes.

Diagram 19 ignores local colour but embodies those lighter patches which appear to shine on the living animal. These are, in healthy specimens, sometimes very apparent and are, of course, formal in quality. That is to say, a rounded part reflects light at some point and thereby evidences its roundness. Darker portions will be seen in the diagram which suggest either the 'raked' or undercutting areas. The horns and toes also show the 'flashes'.

This figure clarifies, or informs on, those matters relative to structure, and analysis of this kind is helpful to the designer.

Now, all drawings attempt to combine (in different proportions) the two textures given in Diagrams 18 and 19. The design of gazelles at the commencement of this chapter is an example of the combining of several facts of both kinds and, though such combination is not essential, it can only be successful should one be able to separate the several significant factors.

Diagram 20 gives a combination of the two upper sets of textures and, though unrelated to surroundings, demonstrates the richness of such possibilities.

The design is reversed in order both to accommodate it better and to present it more freshly to the spectator, but it corresponds in detail to the earlier drawings

184

18.

19.

20.

Colour, or the peculiar markings of the kind, will suffice in rendering many of the more picturesque animals.

The three examples seen opposite, except for the ringing of horns and a little accenting in ears and on the nostrils, depend on colour for their characterisation.

Diagram 21 is from the head of a sable antelope, and its long curved horns and tufty mane are peculiar. The horns are ringed, heavier at the bases, and above these butts taper more gradually.

The sable antelope inhabits the more wooded slopes of Eastern Africa.

The Somaliland beina is a near relative to the last, and is seen in Diagram 22. His horns are straighter, though heavily ringed.

With both of these and the following, the *light patches* on face seem to be the positive marks and this 'make up' of the sable antelope is the most meagre.

The gemsbok of Diagram 23 is another handsome creature with a hump and long, heavily-ringed and slightly lyrate horns. He sometimes carries a throat tuft.

The horns of these three species approximate a circular section. They all taper and, whilst that of Diagram 22 has its horns nearly parallel, those of the gemsbok are lyre-shaped and the sable antelope's are curved backwards and nearly parallel.

The setting of the eyes to the side of head, noticeable in all non-predatory animals, is a special feature of antelopes. These, the large ears and sensitive nostrils, endow the animal with remarkable powers of perception.

Very often the local colouring, besides imparting elegance and a textural richness, conveys an apparent modification or amplification of form. This, it will be clear, requires light as contributary, and much entertainment may be had of this camouflaging of form. The well-known slimming effect of black silk stockings

186

21.

22.

23.

and the tall clown's device of striped clothes are but two examples of the influence colour might play in disguising form.

The beautiful harnessed antelope, whose hoofs are sometimes elongated by residence in swampy tracts, gets its name from its light 'trappings'. The horns are spiralled and flattish in section, face glands are present and his form is that of the normal antelope.

Diagram 24 shows this, and if pigments were used, he would be coloured a rich strawberry with a lighter patch on cheek. A dark brown muzzle, with several white 'straps', and dark brown to black markings on the legs, short mane and the tail enhance one of the loveliest of the antelopes. The white chest band, lips and white tufts in the ears, as also the white emphasis to the black tail tuft, are seen in the diagram as decorative features.

Diagram 25 is from a nylghai. Its peculiar structure has been noted already, but the colour is significant. He is one of those creatures which seem to reverse the order of tones, and he appears darker on the underside than above.

Mention has been made of bony axes determining the attitude, but here is an example of colour effecting attitude, or at least creating an illusion.

This nylghai seems flatter in the body than he is really and his legs appear as being more immaculate than they are. Also, the apparent creases in the neck are not creases but lines of brindled hair. The lighter grey on lower jaw and cheek suggest form which is far different. Surprise touches are seen in the mottled mane and throat tuft as well as in the spots and flecks of white on lower jaw, knee, belly and pasterns.

He is a brindled grey, light and dark, and the seeming creases in neck are made by hairs which are pale where they attach and darker to the outsides.

The bush buck of Diagram 26 is a pretty creature and it will

24.

25.

be noticed that this particular example has been reared on hard ground—his toes are very upright. The peculiar antelope type is seen again in this: quarters are high and tail is short. The choice spotting on the front of quarters and on hinder ribs accords with the remaining delicate colouring and small horns in a charming original.

The oryx, which are of the gemsbok, have scimitar-like horns in some species.

The Soudanese variety (Diagram 27) is pale in colour with richer brown markings on the face, neck and outsides to limbs. Like so many of the antelopes, his head shows a different silhouette from what might be expected.

Acquaintance with the side views only of gnus, hartebeest and gemsbok would lead one to suppose quite other front views from those real ones. It comes as a surprise when investigating a gnu, for instance, that his head, from *frontal* to lower jaw, is so much deeper than it is across from *orbit* to *orbit*.

Possibly, it is this element of surprise which contributes so largely to one's visual enjoyment in these forms.

Colour is held to be of great expressional value when drawing such momentary attitudes given in the turn or twist of a head, the pricking up of ears, and the widening or closing of the eyes. In connection with the last, mention must be made of the eyelashes of animals of the non-predatory kinds. These are often long and thick. They give the effect of softening the large eyes of the hollow-horned and are very noticeable in some species.

The diagrams on page 187 all show eyelashes.

Diagram 28 gives a few notes of a young female reed buck.

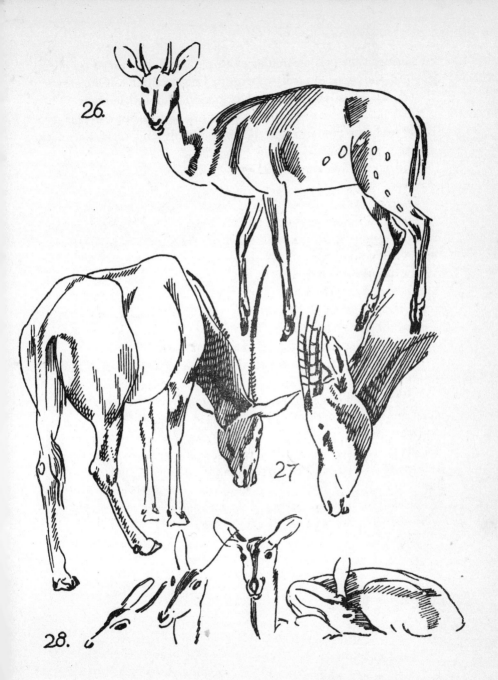

26.

27

28.

Chapter 9

Birds: Waders, Walkers, Predatory, Aquatic

TRUE AS IT MAY BE, FROM THE DRAUGHTSMAN'S POINT OF view, that living animals must be studied when captive or domesticated, it is even more necessary with the feathered kinds.

Timid or otherwise, the wild bird does not permit of close examination except under unusual circumstances. Most bird draughtsmen have had to be content with dead or stuffed specimens and photographs for their study. Increasing knowledge will enable one to utilise the momentary glimpse or most fragmentary information and, in the way that the biologist will reconstruct from a fossilised fragment, a practised draughtsman can visualise and construct an attitude.

It will be unnecessary to remind the student that first-hand acquaintance only will lead him to complete understanding. Structure and functions will be examined in connection with habits and coloration, but the broad principles of anatomy and feather grouping must be appreciated before the drawing from life can proceed very far.

Whether one regards birds as originating on the fifth day of creation or to have evolved from a more primitive form of life, the life history of birds will disclose many truths common to the various families. For instance, birds having rudimentary wings, such as the penguin, emu and ostrich, all bear traces of having flown at some period. All birds are hatched from eggs; and, whilst the parents do not always assist in the hatching or in the feeding and care of the young, they do, when mature, resemble in appearance and habits the stock from which they are sprung.

The main volume of a bird is composed of a compact egg-shaped mass.

At the blunter end of this egg is a cone. This is held at an angle which is best suited to that tilt of the longer axis of the egg and a smaller egg-shape is inserted into the lesser end of the cone. To the pointed end of the large egg is affixed a shovel-like form.

These four parts are seen in Diagram 1. Assembled, they symbolise the bird form with the wings closed to the body. A supporting stilt has been introduced which gives the axes of two parts of the leg.

Diagram 2 shows an end on view of the last—seen from the front—and modelling has been added to both in order to show the overhung or undercutting portions of surface.

Diagram 3 gives a different arrangement of the bird forms, and the leg axes as well as the tilts of head, neck and tail are seen to suggest a new attitude.

Diagram 4 shows projected front view of the last diagram.

Diagrams 5 and 6 give another attitude, and the tail is seen to be dropped onto the central tilt line of body in 5.

The points of attachments of stilts in these diagrams correspond to the knee joint, and the dotted axes show approximate balance of the several parts in a bird.

No particular kind is shown in the six facing diagrams.

Different habits of feeding must develop different parts of the bird but, notwithstanding the increased proportions of some parts and the more rudimentary nature of others, the main structure will conform to the simple arrangements opposite.

The chief organs of flight are the wings, though the tail

194

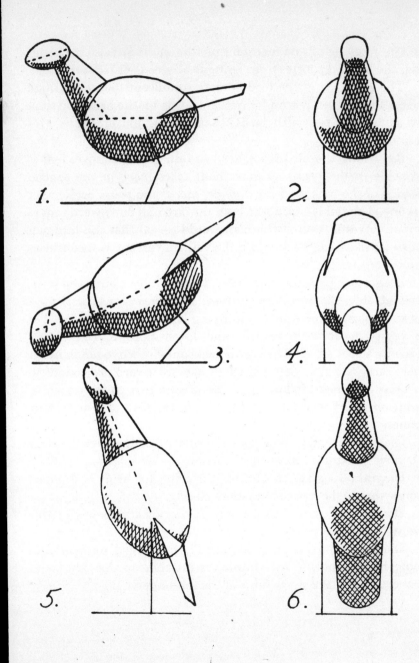

1.

2.

3.

4.

5.

6.

assists in balancing and maintaining him in the air: also in changing the bird's activities from flying to alighting or *vice versa*.

The *underline* of the bird is more significant than the line of back: there is less reason for concentrating on the back line than with animals for, with birds, there is less movement in this region.

Regarding the bird from head to tail, greatest movement is possible in the neck; no movement takes place in the central region of the back, and the *lumbar*, *sacral* and *pelvic* regions act as one. The tail is capable of both upward and downward movement. Investigation of the plan would reveal that the bird can turn its head and neck while the tail movement is inconsiderable.

Diagram 7 gives the bony axes of a generalised bird seen from the left side: the limbs are omitted. The *sternal* (or breast) bone is an important feature and, in flying birds, it is 'keeled'. It has a projecting-forward central and lower portion, resembling broadly a boat's keel. The *dorsal* backbones (seven to ten in number) carry the ribs. Some of these have rearward projections to overlay the next following. Ribs are in two parts, *vertebral* and *sternal*. The neck may have from thirteen to twenty-four bones.

Diagrams 8 and 9 show plan and side of head; and the central 'hollow' of skull is interesting.

Diagram 10 gives the limbs: the wing (or arm) is dropped somewhat to show the bones more clearly.

Diagram 11 shows normal *overlaying* of arm bones in this view.

Diagram 12 gives detailed 'hand': the ordinal numbers denote hand bones. T (or thumb) is attached to the first hand bone; $P\,1$ and $P\,2$ show joints of the forefinger.

196

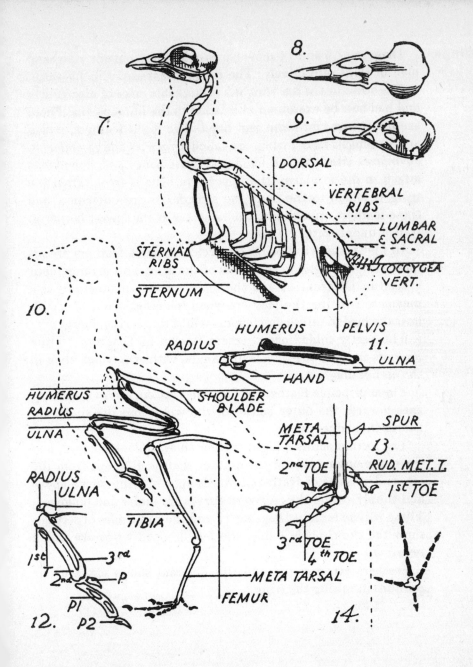

7.

8.

9.

DORSAL

VERTEBRAL
RIBS

LUMBAR
& SACRAL

STERNAL
RIBS

COCCYGEA
VERT.

STERNUM

10.

HUMERUS

PELVIS

RADIUS

11.

ULNA

HAND

HUMERUS
RADIUS

SHOULDER
BLADE

META
TARSAL

SPUR

ULNA

13.

2nd TOE

RUD. MET. T.

RADIUS

1st TOE

ULNA

TIBIA

1st
T
2nd

3rd

P

3rd TOE

Pl

4th TOE

META TARSAL

12.

P2

FEMUR

14.

Diagrams 13 and 14 show bones of left foot (outside view) and plan of right respectively. The top of Diagram 14 is 'forward'.

The structure of the wing is a remarkable piece of mechanism and had best be examined in relation to the human arm. There are upper arm, fore arm and hand. The flight feathers, which are the longest in the wing, are called *primaries* and *secondaries*. *Primaries* attach to the hand and wrist bones and *secondaries* attach to the fore arm: the upper arm bone is free. When the wing is folded to the body the *secondaries* are outermost and those feathers attaching to the hand are at the lowest border as well as underneath.

In flight, the wing being outstretched, these feathers are almost at right angles to the bones of the arm. This arrangement is seen in Diagram 15 and the ligament shown functions as a means of twisting the feathers when 'planing'. This device allows the bird to utilise air currents whilst conserving energy.

The partly folded arrangement is seen in Diagram 16 and feathers are now at a more acute angle, with arm bones, than in the earlier diagram.

These principle feathers of the wings are curved in their long axes towards the outer border of the wing; and the shafts are nearer that edge.

The section across a flight feather shows a double curve, and the curve on one side of the quill or shaft is different from the other. The sides of feathers towards apex of wing curve above and simply, while the rearward curves are under and hollowed. These will be seen in Diagram 17 and the right sides of sections show the *distal barbs* whilst the left dropped *barbs* are called *proximal*.

Feathers act as vanes and this diagram shows effect of air pressure in raising the wing.

198

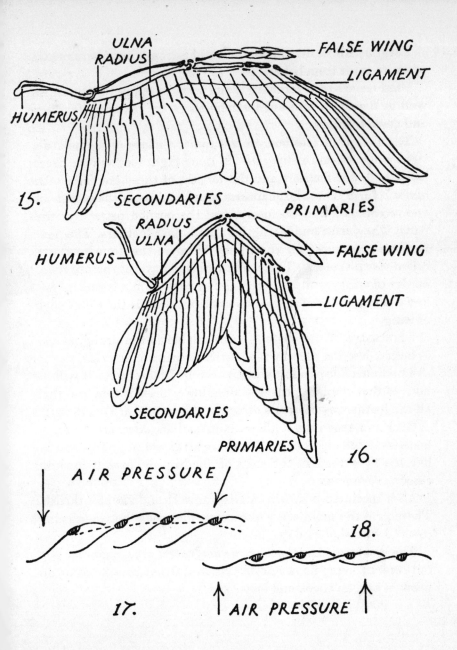

ULNA
RADIUS
FALSE WING
LIGAMENT
HUMERUS
15.
SECONDARIES
PRIMARIES

RADIUS
ULNA
HUMERUS
FALSE WING
LIGAMENT
SECONDARIES
PRIMARIES
16.

AIR PRESSURE

18.

17.
AIR PRESSURE

Diagram 18 shows the sections of beating wing feathers and pressure of air from below.

Feathers are of several kinds and serve as many functions. As well as the flight and tail feathers there are covering feathers and down feathers.

The design of feathers on the upper surface of a mallard's right wing is seen in Diagram 19. Long flight feathers are overlayed by lesser feathers and the longest of these are called the *major coverts*. These large *coverts* equal in number the *primaries* and *secondaries* and, so to say, seal the opened pattern of the wing. They assist and strengthen the longer feathers. The next feathers or groups (for there may be more than one row) are called *median coverts*. These are overlayed towards the *proximal* border of wing, whilst the remaining rows of *minor coverts* follow the original arrangement—curving towards the *distal* edge of wing.

Knowledge of this system is invaluable to the draughtsman as he can describe thereby the particular wing or attitude.

The underside of a left wing is seen in Diagram 20. It will be noticed that the large coverts come lower on this side and that all the feathers overlay in a direction the reverse of Diagram 19.

Over and above the quill or shaft feathers there are covering feathers to the bird's body. These are arranged in groups which, like the hair tracts in the coats of quadrupeds, permit greatest ease in movement.

A set specimen is shown in Diagrams 21 and 22, of a thrush. These give the main areas of *coverts*, the spaces between being covered with shorter down feathers.

The diagrams show back or *median covert* area, shoulder and tail *coverts*, neck, flank and leg *coverts*. Other *coverts* occur on head, at eye, on cheek and lower jaw.

200

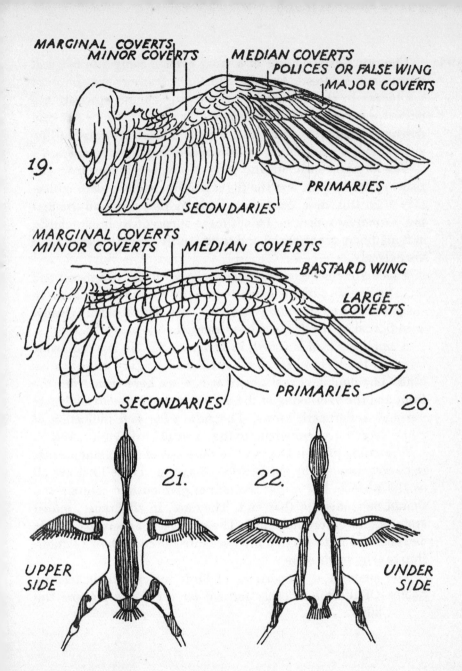

MARGINAL COVERTS
MINOR COVERTS
MEDIAN COVERTS
POLICES OR FALSE WING
MAJOR COVERTS

19.

PRIMARIES
SECONDARIES

MARGINAL COVERTS
MINOR COVERTS
MEDIAN COVERTS
BASTARD WING
LARGE COVERTS

PRIMARIES
SECONDARIES
20.

21. 22.

UPPER
SIDE

UNDER
SIDE

The complex structure of a wing gives a composite of great beauty and subtlety. And the stiff flight feathers are the most significant in the outline. A spread wing curves upwards and outwards towards tips of *primaries*, as well as backwards and downwards from front to rear. This is difficult to draw in line alone, though made easier by the subdividing flight feathers.

The foreshortened curving wing of a pigeon is seen from the rear in Diagram 23, and the flight feathers radiate more noticeably from this view. *Secondaries* overlay *forwards* and the first few *primaries* separate. This is more apparent with some birds, and members of the raven and crow family show this separation very clearly.

A side view is given in Diagram 24 with the wing seen end on. The double curve is expressed by the quality of radiation in the *primary* and *secondary* wing feathers. The bird is alighting, as indicated by the dropped head and tail.

A small sea bird is shown in Diagram 25. He is a Sandwich tern and the webbed feet and 'swallowed' tail are proper to his kind. The double curvatures of wings are here seen from the front and the overlaying of the *primaries* and *secondaries* denote top and underneath views. The *false wing* and indication of *major coverts* give convexity to the curve of bird's right wing.

The strong lines in Diagram 26 show sets of complementaries, in curves, implied by the previous diagram. These lines are all *on* the surface, but might sometimes give outline contour and should be studied to that end. They are, in this sense, *inlines* and, therefore, foreshortened. The strongest of them are visible and active; and the dotted lines are introduced to show relationship to original drawing.

The anatomical proportions of birds indicate their feeding habits. Of those noticeably formed for a definite purpose the

202

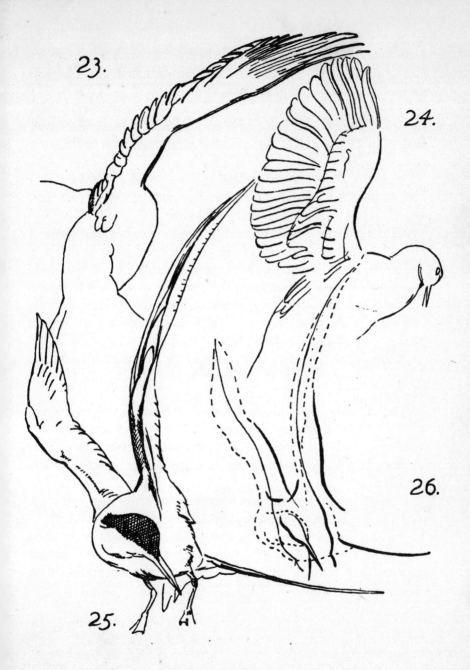

23.

24.

26.

25.

waders and allied kinds are remarkable. The walking feet with strong developed toes are as useful to the bird as the long beak is dangerous to small amphibians.

This family comprises the redshanks, curlews, plovers, storks, herons, bitterns, etc., and one of its members, a grey phalarope, is seen in Diagram 27. The peculiar running action is common to the smaller waders.

Diagram 28 gives an underside view of the left foot of a wader: note the extended first toe. The normal axis of foot (forwards) is to diverge from centre outwards.

All these birds are flight birds as well as waders and some of them migrate extensively. They are included here as showing the great development of the posterior limbs. The stilt-like appearance of these comes from the increase of the lower bones; for the *femur*, whilst strong, is not, comparatively, long.

Diagram 29 shows a sarus crane. He is not a true wader, though sometimes a walking bird.

A Stanley or paradise crane is seen in Diagram 30; and the lengthened secondaries to the inner border of wing are a special feature.

The smaller, black-necked crowned crane is a picturesque bird and his long neck coverts and black head combine surprisingly with his crown of thin, blob-ended feathers of pale amber. The action of Diagram 31 suggests the insect or worm watcher.

Cranes are said to do much damage to crops and are, supposedly, herbivorous, though they are insect eaters too.

For the draughtsman's purpose action or attitude is the most profitable study and, although anatomy must control structure and feather texture contribute likeness, the animation of a drawing is essential.

In drawing all animate life, the designer's job is to select those attitudes most pregnant with meaning. The novice concentrates on idea or information of a literal (or literary) insignificance. The trained draughtsman with an unspoiled vision (and this is not an impossible combination) should choose the most meaningful moments of an action.

A few diagrams on page 207 describe certain attitudes which, though momentary in the originals, have become sufficiently static in the drawings to justify them as illustrations of action.

Diagram 32 shows a Stanley crane preening its shoulder coverts while resting on the ground. The sweeping throat and breast feathers combine in a creature of great elegance. His natural colours are pale—dove grey to darker grey and black in the longer wing and tail feathers—and he has a powdery head, somewhat like a puff.

Diagram 33 shows a love-making dance of the same bird, and the curious wings are spread. The prancing is fantastic, and this drawing summarises the action though avoiding the arrested movement common in the photographic snaps.

Diagrams 34 and 35 give other Stanley cranes; the actions are usual but the designs are expressive—with the minimum of means they are adequate and consistent.

34 augments the twist of the attitude in the indication of legs; the right one strutted and the left one implies the bending of the hidden knee.

35, besides showing the curious head, gives a not uncommon action of the legs.

The white-necked crane of Diagram 36 is after worms and his action is of walking.

It must be divulged that first hand drawings of this kind do

32.

33.

34.

35.

36.

not always 'come off' and a good deal of fortitude and philosophy
are required by the student of bird life drawing.

Indulgence in the calligraphic drawing of the previous page,
pleasant as it is for the executant, should not deter one from a
steadier sort of drawing, and no preference is suggested or de-
sirable—the two are different. Steady investigation of details
might be done in the museums from good examples; and one's
acquaintance with living subjects will soon give discernment in
the choice of set specimens.

Some of the diagrams opposite were drawn from arranged
dead birds and, waiving the inevitable transmutation which
takes place, these provided likely enough subjects.

Predatory birds are strong in flight, have heavy curved beaks
and largish strong feet: their powerful pinions are composed of
well-defined feathers, the eyes are placed to look forward and
their feet are marked boldly with large scales. Eagles, hawks,
kites, falcons, buzzards and owls are in this family: vultures and
condors are more carrion eating than preying birds.

Diagram 37 shows a S. American condor with wings spread
ready to 'take off' in flight. His face and neck are bare and he
wears a ruff of soft white downy feathers. The strong pinions
make a beautiful design in infinite curves and the eye is expressed as facing more forward than with the non-predatory
kinds.

Diagram 38 gives a side view of the condor in a typical roost-
ing attitude and Diagram 39 gives his feet. These are not so
strongly curved in the claw as with the true preying bird nor are
the scales so well marked.

Diagrams 40 and 41 show the peculiar predatory foot—top
view of right foot and under view of left foot respectively—of an
osprey.

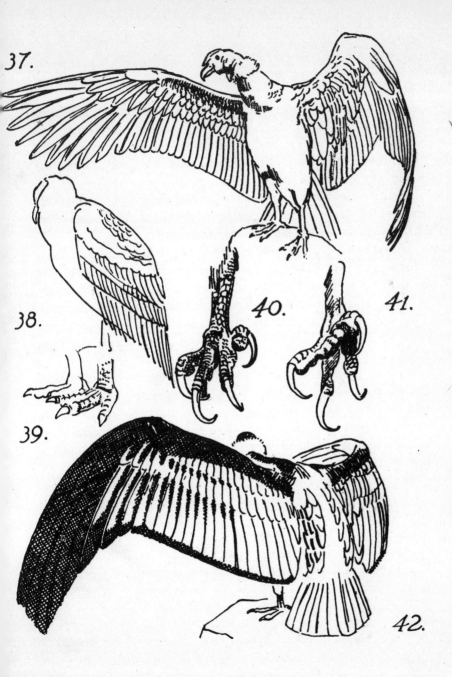

37.

38.

39.

40.

41.

42.

A back view of the condor is given in Diagram 42. The tail shows the normal design, having one feather in the centre to seal this fan.

The textures of feathers and feet introduced in the diagrams of the previous page might suggest a means of amplifying and beautifying a drawing, and the local colour patterning on the individual feathers sometimes provides a rich design, quite independent of their shapes.

Mention has been made of the formal design of the feathers and, whilst these are entertaining in detail, their massed effect will always define the dimensions of the bird.

Diagram 43 is descriptive of a shag or green cormorant. He is a fisher and his webbed feet and beak proclaim his element and natural food. This bird has a glossy covering and the shine, or flash, is responsible for formal definition in the diagram. The darkest tone is put over the shadow areas and so confirms both the shape of bird and the direction from which the light comes.

Swimming and diving birds all have somewhat elongated trunks and *pelves*; the knee joints are restricted in movement and feet are lengthened. Penguins are remarkable in having reduced wings as well. Feet point their centres outwards, the three outside toes are webbed between; in the single instance of the pelican they are all webbed.

Feet are seen in Diagrams 44 and 45. 44 is a top front view of a wild duck's right foot and the other is a left one seen from the side. There are cushions or pads under each of the *phalanges* or toe bones.

Some birds have strikingly patterned feathers and the combined effect of these, when on the birds, is worthy the draughtsman's study.

210

43.

44.

45.

46.

A black-throated diver is seen in Diagram 46 and the white markings on the throat, the shoulders and wing coverts combine to describe both the kind and the attitude.

Colour plays an important part in one's cognizance of birds and not the less, therefore, recognition of attitude.

Everyone is familiar with gulls and they may be seen in town and country as well as by the sea. The great black-backed gull is not uncommon and he is both fisher and scavenger. Like all gulls, he is a strong flier and the length of wing is shown in both Diagrams 47 and 48. The wide stout fan of the tail is another indication of his powers in flight and the big curved bill is capable of holding and tearing. Colour here is decorative and distinctive and 47 is in the position ready to 'take off' in flight, or of remonstration (gulls are notoriously quarrelsome).

The Siberian teal shown in Diagram 49 is patterned more strikingly than his British cousin; and, in the selection of subjects, one ought to suit the subject to medium. For this reason, although some of the 'quieter' designs in feathered coats are amongst the most beautifully marked, preference has been given to those more pictorially suited. Both this teal and the gull of Diagram 47 show the egg form noticed in the earlier part of the chapter; and the form, in each case, is reminiscent of the shell-covered embryo peculiar to the species.

The feather tracts on breast are indicated by the pattern and it might be remembered that the breast bone is not overgrown by coverts; whilst with the duck there is a 'free' line right down the centre of the neck and crop.

Diagram 50 is the kind of serviceable note which is advocated for the student of live birds and would be amplified as opportunity offered. It is of an Iceland goose which is common in the parks.

212

47.

48.

49.

50.

Chapter 10

Game and Domestic Fowls

IT IS SAID THAT ALL THE GREAT VARIETIES OF DOMESTIC or farm yard fowls derive from the Indian jungle fowl. This, though probably true in a biological sense, might be taken as an indication of its universal or general form—it has remained unchanged. In its all round capacity for flight, walking and feeding and its usual proximity to man, we may take the fowl as being the standard form in our investigation of birds. Chicken, as they are diminutively called, show the generalised bird form: wings are not developed for long flight, legs are not unduly lengthened, bodies are compact, beaks (though serviceable) are undeveloped and their feet are still walking feet.

All game birds are closely related to the domestic fowl and, except for slight modifications or developments, the likeness can be traced very easily. Peafowl and pheasants are, perhaps, the closest in form and structure. Afterwards come partridges, grouse, guineafowl and quails: turkeys were the original American representatives.

With the game birds, cocks differ from the hens in form and colour and the males are very ornamental and savage fighters. It seems a rule of dictatorial nature that the most distinctive males vie for supremacy, and polygamy is by no means a deterrent. The cock partridge is not so strongly distinguished in colour from the hen, nor is he polygamous.

Pigeons, as would be expected of such an universal family, are well known in domestication and the common ring dove or wood pigeon is supposed to be the parent stock.

215

Swans, geese and ducks are the remaining kinds grouped in the term domestic fowls. The domesticated aquatic birds have the usual restricted movement of knee joint and are web footed. The bills are wide and the ganders and drakes more striking, in colour and marking, than their mates. These birds have larger heads than the 'chickens' though grace, if not elegance, is shown in the necks of some. Necks are longer than with the cock: cocks have fourteen neck bones, swans twenty-three, geese eighteen and ducks fifteen bones. The *dorsal vertebræ*, again, are most numerous in the swan, which has ten; both goose and duck have nine each and the cock has only seven back bones in this region. As the ribs are attached to these *dorsal* back bones, the bodies of the aquatic birds must be longer than with the cock.

The design of a bird should have, besides the symmetry of the two sides, proper relationship of the lines of back and underneath. The underneath line is very important in itself; for many changes take place in this line, significant as it is of movement and direction.

Excepting only a line which bounds a flat plane, no outline is descriptive of edge alone. Sometimes a salient feature will be expressed by it and, again, a wide and flattened surface might be bounded by the line at any one of several distances. *Underlines* could be simple or clean where a rounded projection occurs and heavier or modelled where symbolising greater surface or mass.

Diagram 1 shows an underline, darkened to convey different features. It gives a young wild duck and the wing has been simplified in order to show the underline.

Diagrams 2 and 3 show underlines of different attitudes and the qualities of expression in the underlines will be seen in the slighter key drawings.

216

1.

2.

3.

That feathers are different in texture, colour and function, might decide one to study birds from the outside, in contradistinction to that inside approach dictated by a knowledge of anatomy. And, after a scrutiny of the proportions and action, it would be a wise decision to analyse the surface groups.

Diagrams 4, 5 and 6 are from a red jungle fowl and show superficial feather groups.

Diagram 4 gives the three-quarter rear view which is repeated in the other two diagrams; and the neck, shoulder and tail coverts are seen to be separated from the darker areas of wing, legs and tail. Short strokes on the neck, shoulder and back are diagrammatic of median or centre lines to feathers; and these are directional. The wing and tail feathers are defined. Notice should be taken of the overlaying of tail feathers—from the bottom upwards on the outer side and *in reverse* for the underside: the feathers increase in length as they rise to the apex of tail.

Diagram 5 shows the extension of tail coverts onto wedge of tail—the 'draped' tail *coverts* are 'festooned'. The central *shafts* of the wing and tail feathers have been introduced.

The tufted appearance of the neck and hood is given by the coloration on the feathers. These are rich dark brown down their centres and edged with orange or yellow.

Coverts round or smooth the form and their grouping must conform to the understructure, whether body, wing or tail.

Diagram 6 gives the completed cock, with his soft, drooping or stiff feathers patterned. The element of roundness or solidity is achieved by the placing of the lines of feathers in this conformation and infinity is suggested by the additional local colour decoration.

A cock jungle fowl is seen in the analysis on page 221.

4.

5.

6.

Diagram 7 shows the direction and order of the flight feathers as seen from the rear. The *primary* wing feathers are long, and their *distal* borders are exposed. The *secondary* flight feathers are piled closely on top of each other. The whole wing conforms to the curvature of the body and the elliptical hole between the two wing extremes shows the shape of tail insertion.

Diagram 8 gives the wedge of tail and it will be noticed that, as the wings are longest at their tips (below), the tail is longest at its apex (above). Again, the tail feathers separate slightly and radiate outwards and downwards from tail attachment. The topmost, or apical, feathers are extended and curving. These tail feathers have their shafts, or quills, placed more centrally than those of the flight feathers.

Diagram 9 shows the symmetry of shoulder, back and tail *coverts* whilst Diagram 10 gives the patterning of these.

Diagram 11 is the assembled bird and the relative values of colours are applied. This view is from rather below, but a clear diagram of feet is seen: the first toes are off the ground and the direction of spurs should be noticed.

The tassels, which hang from the junction of beak and face, are part of the *wattles* and are peculiar. The comb, also, is a special feature and its introduction into a drawing should give character and expression to the bird.

Comb, wattles, neck coverts and extended feathers of tails and wings were appendages which might have made the fighting cocks vulnerable and, as sources of danger, were cut away by breeders.

A 'game cock' is seen at the front of this chapter, and his clipped wing and tail feathers are, structurally, communicative.

An interesting example of reverted domestic fowl is seen in Diagram 12.

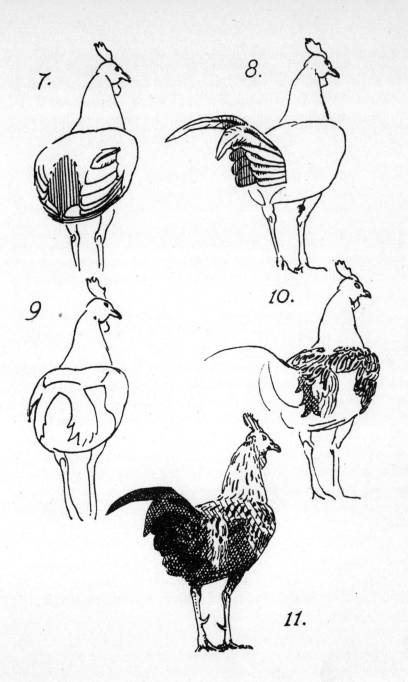

7.

8.

9.

10.

11.

Early voyagers to the Fiji Islands carried individuals of cultivated breeds; some escaped and reassumed the character of their original stock. They resemble somewhat the appearance of the Indian jungle fowl, are smaller than the selectively bred fowl and their colouring is normal or constant. Feather texture is shown in the diagram and the tail is peculiar to the cock family.

The feathers of non-flight birds, such as the ostrich, emu, cassowary, etc., differ from those of the flight birds. Flying birds have feathers of a uniform type, if different in size and colour, and these are distinguished by having a *quill* or *shaft*, sometimes an *after shaft*, *barbs* and *barbelles*. The *barbs* attach to the *shaft* or *after shaft* and the *barbelles* are the minute hooks and scrolls which ensure the neatness of a feather and, consequently, the composite forms of wing, tail and body.

Some feathers have down on the *main shaft* and proper barbs on the *after shaft*. These are usually body coverts, though they may be developed peculiarly by breeders.

A buff Cochin hen is seen in Diagram 13 and the enlarged feathers on legs, the 'puffs' on thighs and the 'frothy' tail *coverts* are peculiar to this fowl. These three kinds of feathers differ from the ordinary wing or body *coverts* and are resembled by the normal feathers of the non-flight birds—they are decorative more than functional. The diagram shows a front view, and textures are intended to suggest both the forms of feathers and species. Feathers on crop and breast have *barbs* on the slight *after shaft* and in this do much to influence the form of the bird.

Animation, which is one of the aims of the draughtsman, will be expressed in the attitude of the subject. Some likely attitudes are shown on the next page and surface form is largely responsible for their definition. Neck coverts are seen to swell the

222

12.

13.

forms in nearly all, though the male birds are most handsome in this respect. Thigh coverts, tails, combs and wattles, as well as the feet, play important parts in this company.

Diagram 14 shows a grubbing cockerel on a windy day; his longer tail feathers are listing to the right.

Diagram 15 is another cock bird answering a distant challenge and his neck is unnecessarily puffed in his impotent ire.

Diagram 16 is one of those irritating birds. Notice his stance in the fury of onslaught.

Diagram 17 gives a feeding hen and contemplative swain: his comb and wattles express a recent twist of the head.

Diagram 18 is a shovelling hen: and the cloud of dust sometimes disturbed by the farm-yard fowl is contributary to the complete expression.

Diagram 19 is of a searcher and his prowl is indicated in the forward foot and bending head.

Diagram 20 is another shoveller. Shaking the feathers is characteristic of the action and the feathers separate in the calligraphic drawing of this bird.

Diagram 21 is a feeding hen. And the final strains of his crowing might be heard from Diagram 22.

Of the game birds, partridges and pheasants most resemble the cock or domesticated 'chicken'. Their legs often carry spurs, their nostrils are bare and the feathers of the male birds frequently differ from those of the hens. Pheasants are more ornamental than partridges and there are many varieties of these. The red-legged partridge is typical of the standard form.

Diagram 23 shows a red-legged partridge: the tail is seen to be shorter than the wing.

Partridges are capable of great powers of flight. The true flight feathers are long and extended towards apex of wing. A

224

14.

15.

16.

17.

18.

19.

20.

21.

22.

left wing is seen from above in Diagram 24 and it will be observed that the first feather is longer than the tenth.

A male of the Lady Amherst pheasant is shown in Diagram
25. He is a strikingly marked bird with black and green on the
head, a black and white ruff, green chest and back, yellow and
orange with black marks on the lower back, blue ends to *primary*
feathers of wing, white and orange with black markings on tail
coverts, greyish-white under with grey-green legs and feet. His
tail carries long feathers of buff with brown markings and the
topmost two are white with black markings.

The pheasants have strong walking feet, armed sometimes
with more than one pair of spurs.

A right foot of a pheasant is seen in Diagram 26. This is a
front view and the first toe is hidden, but one spur is visible.
Note the strong scaling of the foot and leg.

A left wing is seen in Diagram 27, showing the typical *primaries* curve of the pheasant.

A Reeve's pheasant is given in Diagram 28. This bird is decorated in black and brown on a white ground.

It should not be necessary to remind the reader that underneath the feathers are muscles or flesh and bones. (The bony
cage or armature has been detached in detail in Chapter 9 and
all birds conform in the main to the details of the example
given.) What is important, in this working from the outside inwards, is recognition of those things which first influence the
surface.

Those things corresponding to the subcutaneous bones in
other animals must, in the birds also, induce forms or contours
which are normal to the silhouette.

Skeletal portions of a wood pigeon are seen in Diagram 29
and the surrounding contours suggest the flesh and feathers

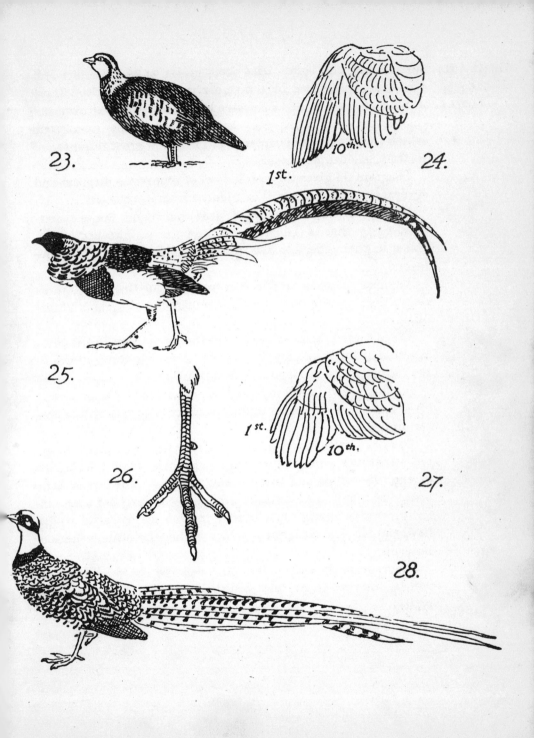

23.

24.

1st. 10th.

25.

26.

1st. 10th.

27.

28.

surrounding the bones. The head, breast, thighs and legs are, obviously, influenced by the underlying bones; and the angle at which the tail is held is dictated by the *coccygeal vertebræ*.

(Comparison of this bony armature with the game cock which introduces the chapter, will prove the great influence of feathers on outline contours.)

Diagram 30 gives the jungle fowl of a previous diagram and several structural facts will be deduced from its contours.

Diagram 31 shows a view of 'arm and 'hand' bones corresponding to that of. Diagram 30; and the significance of the bones in their effecting the outside contours will be acknowledged.

The drop in *pelvis* to rear is responsible for that fall towards tail in the fowl and this might be compared in Diagrams 30 and 32.

The outward thrust of knees and the 'arch' seen in the combination of thigh and leg axes of the latter diagram conform to the normal attitude adopted in Diagram 30.

Q.e.d. written here might well be countered by a *quid nunc* (?) and, for the rest, some actions peculiar to species will be entertaining.

The swan holds his wings in an attitude peculiar. This is adopted sometimes when swimming, sometimes when basking or drying the wings and often when walking. The upper arm bones are raised in an attitude similar to the lurching action of an impressive strong man. It may be that his powerful wings have the biceps development which makes the athlete shorten his arms.

Diagram 33 shows a male mute swan and the *palmate* order will be observed in his feet; whilst the peculiar black wattle is typical.

228

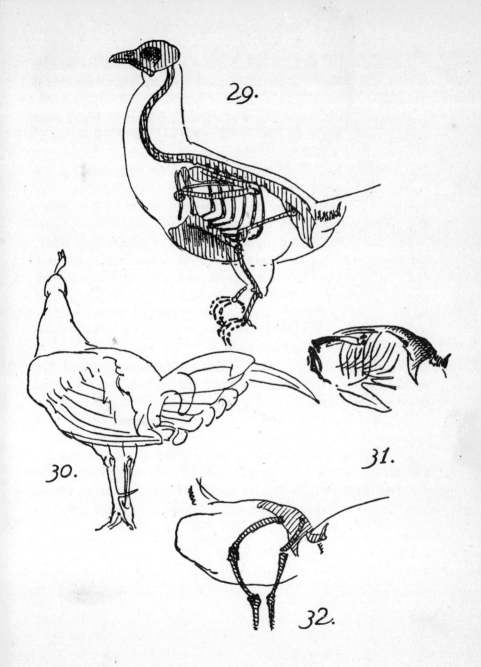

29.

30.

31.

32.

An interesting piece of information about the swan is that he cannot rise in flight from the ground and requires water for his 'take off'.

Diagram 34 is a front view of a duck performing his strange rolling walk. Walking is a difficult art and the duck is handicapped with his stiff knee joints and his elongated outside toes. These fourth toes, as with all birds, have four *phalanges* or toe bones; but, unlike the walking birds or perchers, these four bones are full long. They are, of course, intended for paddling and his walking gait resembles the overarm stroke of a swimmer.

The fan-tailed pigeon or, as he used to be called, the shaker, is a fancy bird. The elevated fan of his so-called 'tail' is operated like that of the peacock and is really composed of elongated tail *coverts*. Evidence of this is given in the fanciers' description that he may have up to thirty-six feathers in the fan. Eleven to thirteen is the sum of tail feathers and part of the fan at least must be, therefore, composed of *coverts*.

Diagram 35 shows a 'shaker' and his name comes from the peculiar action of shaking the neck. He inflates his crop when amorously inclined.

The student who is aware of the structure and assembly of feathers will be in possession of that knowledge necessary to the rapid notation of moving forms. He will never put on a tail upside down or turn the upper surface of a wing inside. His slightest notes will be legible and informative, and assurance must be given that such notes will be entertaining and useful.

230

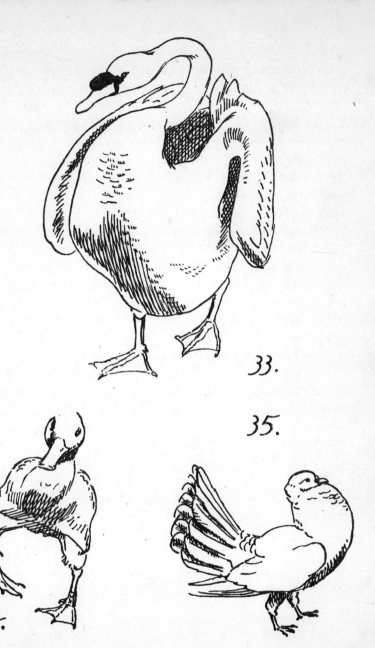

33.

35.

34.